Cosmic Cannabis

Cosmic Cannabis

Matthew Petchinsky

Cosmic Cannabis: Hemp Wisdom from the Zodiac
By: Matthew Petchinsky

Introduction: Stars, Strains, and Sacred Smoke

Since time immemorial, humans have looked to the stars for answers and turned to the Earth for healing. In the vast tapestry of cosmic tradition and botanical wisdom, few combinations feel as intuitively harmonious as astrology and cannabis. Both are ancient systems of understanding—astrology decoding the language of the heavens, and cannabis revealing subtle truths of the self. When fused together, they offer something rare: a deeply personal and often humorous roadmap to who we are, how we feel, and how we evolve.

This book, *Cosmic Cannabis: Hemp Wisdom from the Zodiac*, is a cosmic experiment—an astrological field guide lit with laughter, grounded in cultural wisdom, and dusted with a haze of green insight. It doesn't require you to be an expert astrologer or a cannabis connoisseur. It only asks for your curiosity. Whether you're an Aries rolling into action, a Cancer cocooning in comfort, or a Libra navigating the scales of life with a well-balanced hybrid in hand, this book will meet you where you are—and elevate you just a little higher.

The Legacy of the Stars

Astrology is more than horoscopes and zodiac memes—it is one of humanity's oldest forms of symbolic storytelling. The twelve signs of the zodiac represent archetypes of human behavior, each shaped by elemental forces, planetary rulerships, and the dance of celestial bodies. These signs guide how we act, love, process emotions, and even how we relax and unwind. Each carries a unique energetic blueprint that, when understood, deepens our self-awareness and enhances how we relate to others.

Astrology reminds us that we are part of something bigger. That our moods are tidal, influenced by the moon. That our decisions may echo the movements of Mars. That the way we feel during Mercury retrograde isn't just in our heads. We are stardust—and astrology teaches us to listen to our origins.

The Spirit of the Plant

Cannabis, too, has walked beside us through centuries. It has been used as medicine, as ritual, as food, as fiber, and as inspiration. Long before it was politicized or recreationalized, cannabis was revered for its ability to open doors of perception, soften pain, enhance joy, and foster connection—to the body, to others, and to the divine.

Each strain of cannabis holds a different frequency. Some sharpen the mind, sparking intellectual curiosity and conversation. Others lull the body into rest, making room for dreams and reflection. Cannabis invites us to slow down, to notice more, to laugh a little louder, and to feel a little deeper. In this way, it becomes both mirror and muse—especially when we approach it with intention.

Why Pair the Zodiac with Cannabis?

You might be wondering: what does a Leo's need for attention have to do with Super Lemon Haze? Or how a Pisces' dreamlike temperament might guide their preference for Northern Lights? As it turns out—everything.

Each zodiac sign approaches life with a different rhythm, motivation, and emotional landscape. By understanding how cannabis affects those patterns, we can use it not just for fun, but for alignment. This book explores how each sign engages with the plant—what they love, what they laugh at, how they snack, and what strains best support their energetic makeup. The result is both hilarious and surprisingly insightful.

This is astrology, not as dogma—but as dialogue. This is cannabis, not as escape—but as enhancement. This is about tuning into the natural frequencies of your body, your mind, and the cosmos.

A Journey for All Signs and Seasons

Whether you're a fire sign chasing adventure, an earth sign seeking stillness, an air sign craving stimulation, or a water sign exploring emotional depths—there's a space here for you. Each chapter offers a portrait of one zodiac sign through the lens of cannabis culture, complete with strain recommendations, personality insights, humorous tales, and spiritual side notes.

You'll meet Leos who treat smoke sessions like stage performances, Virgos who keep a spreadsheet of strain effects, and Sagittarians who forget where they put their pipe halfway through a philosophical rant. You'll laugh, learn, and likely see yourself somewhere in the green glow of these cosmic archetypes.

What You'll Find Inside

This book is divided into two parts. Part I explores the twelve zodiac signs and their unique cannabis connections, from preferred strains to their most iconic "high moments." Part II ventures further into the galaxy, offering creative guides for astrological strain pairings, celestial rituals, high horoscopes, moon phase guidance, retrograde remedies, and more.

You'll also find appendices with a curated cannabis strain glossary and a compatibility chart pairing signs with ideal highs—because even the cosmos needs a cheat sheet now and then.

One Rule: Keep It Light. Keep It Lit.

Above all, this is a book of joy. It's meant to celebrate your inner weirdo, your sacred stoner, your cosmic curiosity. It's for the nights you need a laugh, the mornings you want reflection, and the afternoons you need a strain that understands your vibes better than your friends do.

Whether you're a first-time explorer or a seasoned astral traveler, *Cosmic Cannabis* welcomes you into a universe where every sign has its high—and every high has its sign.

So spark up your curiosity, align your intentions, and let the stars be your smoke signal.

This is your journey.
Written in the stars. Sealed in smoke.

Chapter 1: Aries – The Fiery Toker

The Flame That Starts It All

Welcome to the blaze of the zodiac—Aries. As the very first sign in the astrological wheel, Aries charges forward with raw instinct, passion, and unstoppable momentum. Ruled by Mars, the planet of war, drive, and willpower, Aries is the spark of new beginnings—the sign that leaps before it looks and ignites life with fearless enthusiasm.

So what happens when you introduce cannabis into that equation? Fire meets flower. The result? Hilarious, high-powered adventures, bold experimentation, and a snack-fueled crusade that may or may not end with someone trying to microwave cheese on an open Pop-Tart.

Aries at a Glance

- **Element:** Fire
- **Modality:** Cardinal (initiator)
- **Ruling Planet:** Mars
- **Keywords:** Bold, impulsive, energetic, competitive, adventurous
- **Vibe When High:** Fast-talking, hyper-creative, sometimes too daring, always entertaining

Aries approaches cannabis the same way they approach everything else—headfirst and with zero chill. Whether it's trying the strongest edible in the room or challenging friends to a "who can hold the hit longest" contest, Aries doesn't just partake—they dominate. For them, cannabis isn't just for chilling—it's for conquering new dimensions of experience.

Strains That Stoke the Aries Fire

Because Aries is ruled by energy and motion, their ideal cannabis strains tend to be Sativa-dominant or creatively stimulating hybrids. These types of strains amplify Aries' innate zest for life while avoiding the sluggishness that heavier indicas might bring.

◈ Top Strain Picks for Aries

- **Green Crack:** This is Aries in plant form—alert, focused, energized. Perfect for daytime missions, spontaneous creativity, or fast-paced socializing.
- **Sour Diesel:** A zippy classic that powers Aries' need for movement and conversation. Excellent for brainstorming or firing up an impromptu road trip.
- **Jack Herer:** Named after the cannabis activist, this cerebral strain matches Aries' fiery nature with clarity and uplift, while adding a hint of focus.
- **Blue Dream:** A solid backup when Aries needs to cool the jets just slightly. Euphoric, smooth, and just enough relaxation without dimming the inner fire.

Impulses on Fire: Aries' Cannabis Personality

1. The Competitive Toker

An Aries doesn't "just smoke." They compete. Whether it's rolling the tightest joint, taking the biggest dab hit, or turning a lazy afternoon into a joint-rolling tournament, Aries brings adrenaline to the circle. If you light up with an Aries, be prepared to hear, *"Bet you can't handle this strain,"* followed by a coughing fit and a victorious fist pump.

2. The Munchie Gladiator

Once the high hits, Aries enters a culinary battlefield. This sign isn't satisfied with plain chips. They'll attempt to layer nachos, marshmallows, hot sauce, and leftover lasagna in one pan just to prove they can. And they'll challenge you to try it. Spoiler alert: it's surprisingly good—though you'll never recreate it, because Aries didn't measure anything and already forgot the recipe.

3. The One Who's Always Moving

After a few puffs of Green Crack, an Aries might decide to:

- Rearrange the living room at midnight
- Go jogging (in flip flops)
- Launch a YouTube series about cosmic food trucks
- Build a DIY fort with power tools and zero plans
  Their energy doesn't mellow—it just shifts direction. And often that direction is forward, fast, and fueled by determination that may or may not make sense at the time.

The Aries Smoke Session

A typical Aries smoke session feels like:

- A party that starts with one person
- A TED Talk, but about pizza theories
- An unplanned road trip that ends at an abandoned amusement park
- A rapid-fire debate over whether cartoons count as high art

They are rarely the most relaxed person in the circle—but they're always the one who makes things exciting. The moment the joint hits their hand, they become the director of the vibe, the leader of the expedition, and the instigator of the next weird idea.

Aries' High Mishaps: Lessons in Chill

Every Aries toker has a story that begins with: *"Okay, so I may have overdone it..."*

Examples include:

- Eating an entire edible tray despite the warning *"only one square"*
- Getting high and deciding to build a backyard zipline
- Agreeing to attend three parties in one night—and actually trying
- Lighting incense on the stove burner and wondering why it smells like burnt sagebread

Aries' boldness often leads them to push their limits. And while this makes for great stories, it also teaches them (eventually) to temper their fire with a little water—or at least a calming hybrid.

Aries Cannabis Compatibility Tips

- **Best Smoking Buddies:** Gemini (for wild convos), Sagittarius (for spontaneous plans), Leo (for epic energy matches)
- **Needs to Be Patient With:** Virgo (who wants a plan), Capricorn (who brings a checklist), Cancer (who just wanted to cuddle, not build IKEA furniture high)
- **Solo Sessions?** Aries can benefit from solo highs with intention. Cannabis becomes a tool to reflect inward, spark fresh projects, or channel physical creativity—like painting, trail running, or starting a personal vlog series titled *"Blunt Truths with Aries."*

A Final Puff of Wisdom

For Aries, cannabis is never just cannabis. It's an amplifier—a spark that adds fuel to their already-blazing core. It inspires bold ideas, hilarious detours, and moments of unexpected depth. But as with all fire signs, balance is key. When Aries learns to pair their momentum with mindfulness, they don't just blaze—they illuminate.

So to all the Aries out there: light it up, lead the charge, but don't forget to breathe between battles. Even the Ram needs rest—preferably with snacks in hand and a plan (or at least a nap).

Let your flame burn bright—but not out. The universe still has plenty more bowls to pass your way.

Chapter 2: Taurus – The Connoisseur of Comfort

The Earthbound Epicurean

Taurus, the second sign of the zodiac, is ruled by Venus—the planet of beauty, luxury, sensuality, and all things indulgent. Represented by the Bull, Taurus is grounded, persistent, and undeniably drawn to comfort. When paired with cannabis, this Earth sign becomes a master of mellow—transforming the simple act of lighting up into an artful ritual of pleasure and presence.

Where Aries blazes forward in action, Taurus leans back in deep satisfaction. This is the sign that knows how to relax—not because they're lazy, but because they understand that pleasure is sacred. For Taurus, cannabis isn't just about getting high—it's about elevating the experience into something beautiful, rich, and restorative.

Taurus at a Glance

- **Element:** Earth
- **Modality:** Fixed (stable, enduring)
- **Ruling Planet:** Venus
- **Keywords:** Comfort, luxury, patience, sensuality, loyalty
- **Vibe When High:** Grounded, indulgent, slow-moving, deeply content

Taurus is that friend who doesn't just bring the weed—they bring a candle, a velvet blanket, a curated playlist, and a charcuterie board. Everything must feel good, taste good, smell good, and—most importantly—last. Once the Bull is stoned and settled, nothing short of a natural disaster will get them off the couch.

Strains That Indulge the Taurus Senses

Taurus seeks strains that engage all five senses. They aren't just looking for potency—they want quality. Flavor, aroma, texture, and even the aesthetics of the bud matter. This is the zodiac's cannabis sommelier, so don't offer them dry shake or mystery leftovers—they'll quietly decline and roll their own.

◈ **Top Strain Picks for Taurus**

- **Granddaddy Purple:** Rich in grape and berry notes, this Indica is the perfect slow-down companion. It soothes Taurus into a deep, contented state ideal for long evenings and naps mid-conversation.
- **White Widow:** Balanced and earthy, this hybrid offers a calm euphoria with enough clarity to enjoy a luxurious film or deep conversation—without sacrificing Taurus' love for stillness.
- **Gelato:** Sweet, creamy, and flavorful, this strain offers a decadent experience with just the right amount of heady float and body melt. It's dessert in botanical form.
- **Blue Dream:** For Taureans who want a little lift with their relaxation, Blue Dream provides a smooth cerebral buzz paired with comforting body vibes—perfect for creating, daydreaming, or lounging on a sunny balcony.

Taurus and the Art of Leisure

1. The Ultimate Chill Architect

Taurus doesn't light up in chaos. They curate. Their high is an experience—designed with mood lighting, plush textures, and maybe even a scented diffuser. Before the joint is sparked, a Taurus has:

- Adjusted the lighting to warm gold
- Arranged the couch pillows just right
- Selected the perfect post-smoke movie (a visually stunning film, probably set in Tuscany)
- Prepped a snack spread worthy of a magazine photoshoot

Cannabis is not rushed. It's rolled carefully, smoked slowly, and savored completely. Taurus believes in quality over quantity—and they're patient enough to wait for the perfect vibe.

2. The Munchies Maestro

Where some signs panic at the fridge, Taurus transforms it into a culinary playground. Their munchies aren't mindless—they're masterful.

Expect:

- Brie and fig jam on toasted baguette slices
- Dark chocolate dipped strawberries
- Truffle popcorn with pink Himalayan salt
- Or, on "lazy" days: gourmet mac and cheese with breadcrumbs and smoked paprika

They eat with all five senses. Texture, flavor, aroma—it all matters. And yes, they'll share—but only if you don't rush them. A Taurus caught mid-bite is not to be disturbed.

3. The Grounded Guide

While other signs may spiral into abstract thought or chaotic behavior when high, Taurus remains rooted. Their cannabis use is deeply sensory and restorative. They can sit in silence for hours, appreciating the feel of a soft blanket or the taste of a perfect bite. For Taurus, cannabis is a return to the body—and the body, in their view, is sacred.

The Taurus Smoke Session

A Taurus-led smoke session feels like a five-star spa. Everything is thoughtful. The music? Lo-fi beats or acoustic soul. The seating? Cozy, layered, and cushioned. The strain? Smooth, flavorful, tested. They won't start until everything is just right—and once they do, they're not going anywhere.

In the circle, Taurus is often the quiet one, occasionally offering a profound observation or an unsolicited snack from their secret stash. They won't dominate the conversation, but they'll be the one everyone ends up leaning against by the end of the night. Their vibe is calm, nurturing, and unbothered.

Taurus High Tales: The Couch Chronicles

The Gourmet Burnout:

One Taurus decided to experiment with a high-end edible: a lavender-infused dark chocolate bar with 10mg per square. After two pieces, they settled in for what they thought would be a light buzz. An hour later, they were found cocooned in six blankets, whispering to a bowl of grapes and rating them by mouthfeel and emotional resonance.

The Unmovable Object:

Another Taurus once got so perfectly comfortable—wrapped in a fleece robe, watching a fireplace video on YouTube—that when a friend asked them to help find the TV remote, they simply whispered, "I live here now," and didn't move until morning.

The Sensory Stargazer:

On a camping trip, a Taurus smoked a mellow indica under the stars and spent three hours lying on a mossy rock, insisting it was the most perfect texture they'd ever touched. "It feels like nature's hug," they murmured repeatedly, as if discovering a secret. They later named the rock Harold.

Taurus Cannabis Compatibility Tips

- **Best Smoking Buddies:** Cancer (cozy energy match), Pisces (aesthetic vibing), Virgo (organized and prepared)
- **Needs Patience With:** Aries (too loud), Sagittarius (too restless), Gemini (too many questions during a movie)
- **Solo Sessions?** Ideal. Taurus thrives in solo highs—candle-lit baths, soft music, plush pajamas, and maybe a snack-tasting journal. Their love language is solitude infused with luxury.

A Final Puff of Wisdom

Taurus teaches us that cannabis isn't just about the high—it's about the *how*. They remind us to slow down, appreciate, savor. In their world, quality is holy, the body is a temple, and the couch is an altar. Their grounded presence helps others feel safe, welcomed, and—if lucky—well-fed.

So to all the Taurus tokers out there: Keep indulging. Keep curating. Keep crafting a life that feels as good as it looks. Because when you're high, the world doesn't spin—it melts into velvet.

Light it slowly. Taste it deeply. And don't forget to fluff your cushions first.

Chapter 3: Gemini – The Social Smoke Butterfly

The Whirlwind of the Zodiac

Gemini, the third sign of the zodiac, arrives like a gust of wind—swift, curious, and always stirring something up. Ruled by Mercury, the planet of communication, language, and thought, Gemini embodies mental agility, humor, and intellectual exploration. Symbolized by the Twins, this sign holds two (or more) personalities in one—constantly oscillating between ideas, moods, and interests.

When a Gemini gets high, things get...lively. One moment, they're texting three friends at once about completely unrelated topics. The next, they're telling a story about a squirrel they met once in college that changed their life. Then they're suddenly deep in conversation with your fiddle-leaf fig plant, nodding seriously as if it's giving them financial advice.

Cannabis doesn't slow Gemini down. It adds fuel to their neural fire—turning a curious mind into a stoned symphony of words, theories, and social chaos.

Gemini at a Glance

- **Element:** Air
- **Modality:** Mutable (adaptable, ever-changing)
- **Ruling Planet:** Mercury
- **Keywords:** Talkative, witty, adaptable, curious, expressive
- **Vibe When High:** Chatty, creative, fidgety, unpredictable

Geminis are natural entertainers, multitaskers, and trivia-lovers. They can turn a chill session into a three-hour podcast or a smoke break into an existential stand-up comedy show. They don't just get high—they explore, perform, debate, and sometimes forget what they were saying mid-sentence (but still land the punchline).

Strains That Sync with Gemini Energy

Because Gemini is ruled by Mercury, they crave stimulation. Sativa-dominant or clear-headed hybrid strains tend to be their best match, enhancing their sociability, mental clarity, and sense of humor without weighing them down.

◈ **Top Strain Picks for Gemini**

- **Sour Diesel:** The ultimate conversation starter. It fuels mental energy, creativity, and quick-fire wit—ideal for debate nights or impromptu storytelling.
- **Jack Herer:** Named after the activist and thinker, this cerebral strain aligns perfectly with Gemini's craving for information and discussion.
- **Durban Poison:** A pure sativa that enhances focus, alertness, and verbal fluency—great for multitasking, texting, or recording an episode of "High Thoughts with the Twins."
- **ACDC (high-CBD):** For Geminis who need to calm the mental chatter without losing clarity. Perfect for introspection or more mindful communication.

The Gemini Cannabis Experience

1. The Smoke Circle DJ

Gemini can't help but control the vibe. They've got the playlist ready (with wildly mismatched songs), a new edible brand to try, and three "must-watch" YouTube videos queued. They bounce from one topic to another with ease, keeping everyone entertained and confused in equal measure. Interrupting themselves mid-sentence is common—and oddly endearing.

2. The Multitasking Muncher

Only Gemini can eat cheesy snacks, text six people, rearrange the coffee table, and explain string theory all while high. They're the ones who:

- Microwave something but forget what
- Try three snacks simultaneously and rate them out loud
- Create an elaborate snack rating scale, then abandon it five minutes later

They're the type to suddenly stand up during a session and say, "BRB—I had an idea!" and return an hour later with a bowl of cereal and a screenplay outline.

3. The Philosophical Tangent Chaser

Gemini + cannabis = hypertext consciousness. Start talking about space and they'll somehow segue into a breakdown of cartoon physics, 17th-century philosophers, and a wild theory that your cat is actually a reincarnated Victorian poet. None of it makes sense—and all of it makes sense.

Gemini's High-Volume Highs

The Talk to Plants Episode:
One Gemini was once so entranced by their cannabis high and a new sativa strain that they began a full-blown TED Talk to their houseplants. Topics included: "How Photosynthesis Changed My Perspective on Hustle Culture" and "Are You Guys Happy in This Corner?" It ended with them applauding the ficus for being such a "strong listener."

The Great Group Chat Debacle:
Another Gemini got high and decided to text everyone they hadn't spoken to in months—resulting in three rekindled friendships, one confused ex, and an invitation to a high school reunion they accidentally RSVP'd "yes" to. They never went, but they did make a playlist for it just in case.

The Twin Tangent Spiral:
While recording a cannabis-fueled podcast about comic books, a Gemini veered off-topic and ended up deep-diving into the politics of gummy bears, the ethics of time travel, and whether or not birds understand sarcasm. The episode gained 3,000 listens and a sponsorship from a snack company.

The Gemini Smoke Session

If you're at a smoke session with Gemini, expect:

- Frequent interruptions that lead to even better conversations
- Spontaneous games or storytelling competitions
- New nicknames by the end of the night (you'll be "Moon Nugget" forever now)
- Lots of laughter and zero silence
- Probably a whiteboard or chalkboard for visualizing ideas nobody asked for

Gemini loves being around people during a session, but they're also fantastic solo smokers—especially when writing, painting, coding, or working on multiple half-finished projects at once.

Gemini Cannabis Compatibility Tips

- **Best Smoking Buddies:** Libra (great convos), Aries (can keep up with the energy), Aquarius (will add to the madness)
- **Needs Patience With:** Capricorn (too serious), Taurus (too slow), Scorpio (who demands emotional depth too soon)
- **Solo Sessions?** Yes—but structure helps. Journaling, puzzle-solving, voice-recording, or live-tweeting high thoughts can keep their inner chaos joyful instead of scattered.

A Final Puff of Wisdom

Gemini isn't here for the slow-and-silent high—they're here to light up and light up the room. Their cannabis journey is all about expression, connection, and curiosity. They remind us that being high isn't always about going inward—it can be a celebration of the world around us and the ideas inside us waiting to get out.

So to all the Gemini tokers: keep talking, keep laughing, and don't ever lose that spark of mischief. Your words are spells. Your laughter is medicine. Your mind is a constellation—and every puff adds another star.

Now pass the joint and tell us what that houseplant said again.

Chapter 4: Cancer – The Moonlit Tokers

The Nurturer of the Zodiac

Cancer, the fourth sign of the zodiac, is ruled by the Moon—the ever-shifting celestial body that governs emotion, intuition, and the rhythm of our inner tides. Symbolized by the Crab, Cancer is the protector of the heart, the keeper of memory, and the builder of sanctuary. This water sign moves through life with sensitivity, depth, and fierce loyalty, always retreating into their shell when the world feels too harsh.

When a Cancer gets high, they don't aim to escape the world—they aim to feel it more deeply. Cannabis magnifies their connection to music, memory, and emotion. With the right strain, a Cancer can transform a simple smoke session into a sacred act of healing, reflection, or togetherness. But beware: they might also start crying about the time their childhood goldfish looked at them "with so much love."

Cancer at a Glance

- **Element:** Water
- **Modality:** Cardinal (initiating emotional energy)
- **Ruling Planet:** The Moon
- **Keywords:** Sensitive, nurturing, intuitive, nostalgic, protective
- **Vibe When High:** Cozy, sentimental, dreamy, emotionally attuned

Cancers are the homebodies of the zodiac, the caretakers, and emotional architects. They light up in familiar spaces, surrounded by people they trust, or preferably alone with a soft blanket, a playlist from 2007, and a bowl of something warm. Their highs are introspective and sensory—guided by comfort, mood, and the urge to cocoon.

Strains That Soothe the Cancerian Soul

Cancer benefits from strains that ease anxiety, enhance introspection, and encourage emotional release without tipping into paranoia. They often favor indica-leaning or hybrid strains that calm the nervous system and support deep inner work—or a good nostalgic cry.

◈ **Top Strain Picks for Cancer**

- **Northern Lights:** A classic indica that relaxes the body and invites Cancer into their dream space. Ideal for softening overactive emotions or unwinding into memory.
- **Blueberry:** Sweet and comforting, this strain offers a soothing buzz with gentle euphoria. Perfect for at-home movie nights or journaling under fairy lights.
- **Granddaddy Purple:** A sedating, soul-hugging strain that helps Cancer release the emotional weight they carry for others. Best when paired with a cuddle pile or plush robe.
- **Bubblegum Kush:** Balanced and playful, this hybrid enhances Cancer's creativity and sentimental side without overwhelming them emotionally.

The Cancerian Cannabis Experience

1. The Comfort Creator

Cancer's ideal smoke space is not a smoke *spot*—it's a **nest**. Think:

- Layers of blankets and pillows
- Candles or moon lamps
- Lavender mist in the air
- A cat curled nearby or a heating pad in their lap
- A nostalgic movie queued up (likely animated or romantic)
  They smoke slowly, reverently, and only after setting the mood just right. Cannabis for Cancer isn't an activity—it's a *ritual of safety.*

2. The Emotional Time Traveler

One puff of Northern Lights and suddenly Cancer is remembering:

- Their first heartbreak
- That one summer road trip
- The exact smell of their grandma's living room

Cancers are deeply nostalgic, and cannabis unlocks emotional memory for them like a key. They'll play old songs and cry with gratitude or scroll through old photos and narrate each one with tearful laughter. It's not drama—it's reverence. They feel everything, and weed only softens the barriers between now and then.

3. The Cosmic Empath

Under the influence, Cancer can become a deeply attuned listener and emotional translator. They pick up on the room's mood, soothe anxious friends, and offer surprisingly profound observations. But if the energy's off? They'll retreat—quickly. Their shell goes up, and only snacks or emotional reassurance will lure them back out.

Cancer's High Moments

The Blanket Fort Oracle:
One Cancer got high with friends, built an elaborate blanket fort in the living room, and declared it "The Healing Shell." Each friend had to enter the fort one at a time and receive a personalized emotional reading. There was soft jazz playing. Everyone cried. It became an annual tradition.

The Memory Loop:
Another Cancer once smoked a mellow hybrid and ended up watching old home movies until 3 AM. Between sobbing over their baby photos and texting their mom "thank you for everything," they also handwrote a letter to their middle school self and left it in the freezer for future emotional emergencies.

The Empath Overload:
During a group session, a Cancer got high and suddenly sensed that one of their friends was sad—even though they hadn't said anything. Cancer sat beside them, held their hand, and said, "I just feel like your heart is tired." The friend burst into tears. Cancer then made tea, fetched a blanket, and hummed a lullaby. The others watched in awe, unsure if they had witnessed a breakdown or a divine intervention.

The Cancer Smoke Session

If you're lucky enough to be invited to a Cancer's smoke session, prepare to feel:

- Emotionally safe
- Fed and nurtured (snacks will be warm and thoughtful)
- Very sleepy by the end
- Possibly like you just attended therapy

The playlist will lean lo-fi, nostalgic, or soulful. Expect dim lighting, deep talks, and maybe a collective "what even is time?" conversation. Cancer doesn't get high just to escape—they want to connect. With you. With themselves. With their memories. With the moon.

Cancer Cannabis Compatibility Tips

- **Best Smoking Buddies:** Taurus (same chill frequency), Pisces (dreamy depth), Virgo (quiet caretaking vibe)
- **Needs Patience With:** Gemini (talks too much), Leo (takes up too much spotlight), Aries (too aggressive with the lighter)
- **Solo Sessions?** Absolutely essential. Cancer thrives in solo highs designed for emotional processing, dreamwork, writing, cooking, or simply snuggling with their emotions in silence.

A Final Puff of Wisdom

Cancer reminds us that being high doesn't always mean being funny, fast, or philosophical. Sometimes, it means *feeling*. Really feeling. The softness of a blanket, the salt in your tears, the glow of a memory, the peace of simply existing.

Cannabis offers Cancer an emotional echo chamber where their inner voice gets louder—and kinder. They find healing not through distraction, but through *presence.* They show us the beauty of staying in, slowing down, and letting it all wash over us like moonlight on still water.

So to all the Cancer tokers: never apologize for your tenderness. It is your superpower. Keep creating safe spaces, building cozy cocoons, and reminding the world that the softest signs often have the strongest magic.

Now pass the bowl and the blanket. It's time to cry-laugh over old cartoons.

Chapter 5: Leo – The Regal Roar

The Sovereign of the Zodiac

Leo, the fifth sign of the zodiac, is ruled by the Sun—the luminous center of our solar system. And like their celestial ruler, Leos shine. Bold, passionate, charismatic, and dramatic, Leo is a fire sign through and through. Symbolized by the lion, they walk through life with a natural sense of authority, style, and unapologetic flair. Wherever they go, they carry the energy of royalty, even if it's just to a backyard smoke session.

When Leo gets high, it's not a private affair—it's an *event*. Whether they're telling animated stories, breaking into spontaneous song, or hyping up the group for an impromptu lip-sync battle, Leos use cannabis like a spotlight enhancer. Their highs are larger-than-life, laughter-filled, and sometimes surprisingly heartfelt. They don't just smoke—they perform.

Leo at a Glance

- **Element:** Fire
- **Modality:** Fixed (sustained energy and loyalty)
- **Ruling Planet:** The Sun
- **Keywords:** Confident, playful, loyal, dramatic, expressive
- **Vibe When High:** Entertaining, affectionate, occasionally theatrical, always radiant

Leo doesn't just want to get high—they want to *elevate the entire experience* for themselves and everyone around them. They see cannabis as a social enhancer, a performance enhancer, and sometimes, even a glamour enhancer. Prepare for themed sessions, curated playlists, and over-the-top snack presentations.

Strains That Light the Leo Fire

Leos seek strains that amplify their natural joy, confidence, and creativity. Sativas or stimulating hybrids tend to work best, fueling their extroverted tendencies and keeping their radiant energy glowing strong.

◈ Top Strain Picks for Leo

- **Super Lemon Haze:** Bright, citrusy, and euphoric—this strain fuels Leo's exuberance and ensures they stay the center of attention all night.
- **Golden Goat:** Sweet, tropical, and artistically energizing—perfect for Leos planning a high-concept party or creative performance.
- **Tangie:** With its uplifting citrus flavor and social buzz, Tangie is Leo's ideal wake-and-bake companion for a day of content creation.
- **Blue Dream:** For those quieter Leo moments (they do exist), Blue Dream offers just enough bliss to keep the fire burning without overwhelming.

The Leo Cannabis Experience

1. The Smoke Circle Star

There is no such thing as "just hanging out" when Leo is high. They turn every session into:

- A comedy set
- A storytime special (with multiple accents)
- A mini-concert
- A dramatic reading of old love texts
- Or a live stream that *somehow* has 500 views in 30 minutes

They light up with intention—and that intention is to *entertain*.

2. The Designer of Vibes

Leo curates every session like a production. Their checklist includes:

- Lights that change colors with the music
- A smoke-friendly outfit that belongs on stage
- Music ranging from hip-hop to Broadway to Beyoncé's live performances
- And yes, a mirror nearby so they can check their aura mid-session

Leo knows that the vibe isn't just what you smoke—it's *how* you smoke it. For them, cannabis is as much about beauty and energy as it is about the high.

3. The Unforgettable Host

Leos take hosting seriously. If you're smoking at their place, expect:

- A grand entrance
- The best seating reserved for you (after they pick their throne)
- A themed snack table ("Zodiac Bites" or "420 Tapas" are real possibilities)
- Party favors (edible gummies shaped like lion paws? Why not?)
- An open invitation to their high-stakes karaoke showdown (you WILL be assigned a song)

Leo's High Tales of Glory

The Karaoke Kings & Queens:
One Leo once hosted a cannabis karaoke night titled *"Hits & Hits: One Joint, One Jam"* where everyone had to draw a song and a strain from two separate bowls. The result? One friend crooning Adele through giggles and another performing a reggae rendition of "Bohemian Rhapsody." Leo, of course, closed the night with a glittery mic and a full-body performance of "Halo."

The Live Stream That Went Too Well:
Another Leo got high and decided to live-stream their "stoner thoughts and makeup tutorial." What started as a joke turned into a viral 3-hour livestream featuring philosophical tangents, cosmic contouring, and a spontaneous monologue about lions being misunderstood introverts. The next day, they woke up to 2,000 new followers and a comment from a brand asking to collaborate.

The Snack Pageant:
A Leo once organized a "Munchies Fashion Show," in which snacks were dressed up in costumes (gummy bears in capes, popcorn "brides," and a Dorito emperor). Each snack strutted down a miniature runway made from rolling trays. Judges were high. Laughter was abundant. The winning snack? A Nutella-covered strawberry wearing a tiny tiara. Leo wept with joy.

The Leo Smoke Session

With Leo, expect:

- Performances (planned *and* improvised)
- Loud laughter
- Group photos that they insist on captioning
- Deep loyalty and compliments that warm your heart
- An unforgettable time—whether you were high or not

They're the life of the party, yes—but they're also incredibly warm-hearted. Leo uses cannabis to connect, to uplift, and to create memories worth retelling. They don't just light a joint—they light up the whole room.

Leo Cannabis Compatibility Tips

- **Best Smoking Buddies:** Aries (bold energy), Gemini (endless banter), Libra (appreciates Leo's taste and drama)
- **Needs Patience With:** Virgo (too structured), Capricorn (too focused on goals), Scorpio (too secretive)
- **Solo Sessions?** Rare, but therapeutic. When alone, Leo may use cannabis to spark creativity, process feelings, or practice a monologue in front of the mirror (yes, they *will* applaud themselves).

A Final Puff of Wisdom

Leo shows us that cannabis doesn't have to be low-key—it can be electric, expressive, and exhilarating. When Leo gets high, the world becomes a stage, and the smoke becomes a spotlight. Yet beyond the sparkle, Leo carries a generous spirit. Their high brings joy not just to themselves but to everyone lucky enough to orbit their flame.

So to all the Leo tokers: keep roaring. Keep glowing. Keep making every moment shine a little brighter—whether you're passing a joint, a mic, or a bottle of glittery THC soda.

The crown fits, the roar echoes, and the stage is always yours.

Chapter 6: Virgo – The Methodical Herbalist

The Precision of the Zodiac

Virgo, the sixth sign of the zodiac, is ruled by Mercury—the planet of intellect, communication, and order. But unlike its Gemini counterpart, Virgo expresses Mercury's energy through structure, discernment, and focused thought. Represented by the Virgin (more accurately, the independent harvest goddess), Virgo is meticulous, health-conscious, and highly analytical. They don't just observe the world—they analyze, refine, and optimize it.

When Virgo gets high, it's not chaotic or whimsical—it's intentional. This is the sign that reads the lab report on every strain, measures out their perfect dose in milligrams, and prepares snacks *before* the session begins. For them, cannabis is not an escape—it's a functional tool for healing, clarity, and controlled relaxation.

Virgo at a Glance

- **Element:** Earth
- **Modality:** Mutable (flexible but detail-oriented)
- **Ruling Planet:** Mercury
- **Keywords:** Analytical, grounded, health-conscious, practical, service-oriented
- **Vibe When High:** Calm, clear, observant, deeply introspective

Virgos are the zodiac's wellness warriors, herbalists, and ritual designers. While others may stumble into a smoke session, Virgo approaches it like a well-researched self-care experiment. They may start with an intention, a light body scan, a journal check-in, and a perfectly curated playlist of calming frequencies.

Strains That Support the Virgo Vibe

Virgos prefer strains that promote clarity, relaxation, and bodily harmony. They may avoid high-THC products unless they've studied their effects firsthand. Virgo gravitates toward balanced hybrids, high-CBD strains, and anything with a clean, clear terpene profile.

◈ Top Strain Picks for Virgo

- **Harlequin:** A high-CBD strain that allows Virgo to unwind without losing focus. Ideal for managing anxiety, inflammation, or overthinking.
- **ACDC:** Virtually no psychoactive effects, but deeply calming for body and mind—perfect for Virgo's wellness rituals.
- **Cannatonic:** Another balanced option with a gentle buzz, offering physical relief and mental clarity. Great for creative Virgo types or those easing into cannabis.
- **Blue Dream:** For moments when Virgo wants a little more lift without losing control, Blue Dream offers a euphoric but functional high.

The Virgo Cannabis Experience

1. The Planner of Highs
Virgo doesn't "just get high"—they *schedule* it. They plan:

- What time to smoke
- What dosage to use
- What strain pairs best with their desired outcome (relaxation, creativity, sleep)
- What snacks to prepare (healthy options only—or upgraded classics)

They might even pre-portion their edibles and label them with effects like: "Evening use only – promotes lucid dreams."

2. The Mindful Muncher
While others devour snacks without a second thought, Virgo eats with intention. Expect:

- Organic fruit sliced and arranged in ascending size
- Dark chocolate infused with adaptogens
- Homemade almond flour cookies (with balanced macros)
- Or if they *must* have junk food: air-fried nachos with finely chopped greens hidden beneath the cheese

They're not judging your pizza rolls. But they *did* bring flax crackers with cannabis-infused hummus, just in case.

3. The Ritual Designer

Virgo treats cannabis like part of a healing toolkit. They might incorporate:

- Breathwork before and after smoking
- Journaling or tarot for reflection
- Skin care masks during the high
- Or a post-session herbal tea to balance the system

They don't just smoke—they integrate. They create harmony between plant and person.

Virgo's High Moments of Mastery

The Dosage Spreadsheet:
One Virgo built a personal Google Sheet to track every strain they've tried. Columns included: THC/CBD %, terpene profile, onset time, peak time, mood effects, snack cravings, and post-high productivity rating. It later became a blog. With citations.

The Cannabinoid Cleanse:
Another Virgo combined cannabis with a 7-day wellness retreat they created for themselves. Activities included daily yoga, full-spectrum tinctures, guided journaling, vegan meals, and CBD soaks. By the end of the week, they claimed their soul felt "cleaner than a lab flask."

The Infused Meal Prep Guru:
A Virgo once batch-prepared three days of cannabis-infused meals with carefully calculated microdoses. The meals were anti-inflammatory, gluten-free, and color-coded for digestion. They also provided recipe cards with strain pairings and suggested meditation tracks.

The Virgo Smoke Session

If you're invited to Virgo's session, know this:

- There will be a clean table with rolling trays, wipes, and pre-rolled joints
- Glass will be spotless. Lighters arranged symmetrically.
- They'll offer you water (with lemon)
- There may be a conversation checklist—yes, they prepared questions
- The entire experience will feel like a spa treatment with scientific undertones

They'll ask how you feel, adjust the dose if needed, and probably remind you to hydrate. You'll leave feeling seen, soothed, and strangely more organized.

Virgo Cannabis Compatibility Tips

- **Best Smoking Buddies:** Taurus (enjoys the detail), Capricorn (loves systems), Cancer (appreciates the care)
- **Needs Patience With:** Sagittarius (too chaotic), Gemini (too disorganized), Leo (takes over the show)
- **Solo Sessions?** Often preferred. Virgo finds personal highs ideal for introspection, body scanning, planning, or creating systems they can share with others later. They're the type to invent new rituals while high—and actually write them down.

A Final Puff of Wisdom

Virgo reminds us that cannabis can be sacred, structured, and deeply healing. They are the calm within the storm, the editor of chaos, and the curators of clarity. For Virgo, cannabis isn't about rebellion or escapism—it's about integration. A tool. A practice. A plant of purpose.

They show us that being high can mean being *more present*, more aligned, and more thoughtful. They don't lose themselves in the clouds—they organize them.

So to all the Virgo tokers: keep refining your rituals. Keep elevating the experience. Keep showing the world that intention is the most powerful ingredient in any high.

Now pass the CBD tincture. And don't forget—inhale for four counts, exhale for six.

Chapter 7: Libra – The Balanced Blazer

The Harmonizer of the Zodiac

Libra, the seventh sign of the zodiac, is ruled by Venus—the planet of love, beauty, and artistic sensibility. Symbolized by the Scales, Libra is constantly seeking balance: between extremes, within relationships, and especially within themselves. Refined, charming, and aesthetically attuned, Libras are the social diplomats of the zodiac, floating gracefully through conversations, design schemes, and curated playlists.

When a Libra gets high, the experience becomes a performance of harmony. The lighting will be soft, the snacks beautifully plated, and the music well-matched to the vibe. But don't expect them to choose the strain quickly—they'll spend twenty minutes debating between two equally great options, then pick a third one entirely.

Libra at a Glance

- **Element:** Air
- **Modality:** Cardinal (initiates social flow and refinement)
- **Ruling Planet:** Venus
- **Keywords:** Charming, indecisive, balanced, refined, artistic
- **Vibe When High:** Elegant, flirty, deeply thoughtful, delightfully conflicted

Libras are the stoned aesthetes of the zodiac. They don't just get high—they curate a sensory experience. Think: eucalyptus incense, silk throw pillows, perfectly rolled joints in a gold tray, and debates about which classic film should accompany the evening.

Strains That Suit the Libra Aesthetic

Libra seeks equilibrium—not too sleepy, not too intense. They're drawn to hybrid strains that let them feel creative, social, and lightly euphoric, without tipping into couch-lock or overthinking. Bonus points if the strain has a floral aroma or comes in chic packaging.

◈ Top Strain Picks for Libra

- **Lavender:** A fragrant, indica-leaning hybrid that soothes without sedating. Libra loves its floral essence and luxurious effect.
- **Strawberry Cough:** Light, bright, and sociable. This sativa-leaning strain keeps Libra witty and energized—perfect for group sessions or artistic endeavors.
- **Gelato:** Balanced, smooth, and delicious—just like a Libra's ideal vibe. Great for mellow euphoria without losing social clarity.
- **Pink Runtz:** Sweet, calming, and subtly uplifting. This hybrid pairs beautifully with Libra's inner romantic and love of harmony.

The Libra Cannabis Experience

1. The Aesthetic Architect

Libra won't tolerate a messy setup. Their cannabis session will feature:

- Matching rolling papers and ashtrays
- Artful lighting (think string lights or Himalayan salt lamps)
- A charcuterie board with edible THC cheese, or a matcha latte with a cannabis-infused drizzle
- A Spotify playlist named something like *"Stoned in Silk Pajamas"*

They need the visuals to match the vibe. Beauty is part of their high. If the couch cushions are clashing, they'll adjust them before taking a puff.

2. The Indecisive Inhaler

No sign struggles with choice quite like Libra. Expect:

- A 30-minute debate about which movie to watch
- Frequent requests for "your opinion" followed by "I don't know though…"
- A strain selection process that involves reading five Leafly reviews, doing a mini tarot reading, and then going with whatever smells prettiest

Their mind constantly weighs all sides. Even when it comes to snacks, they'll ask, "Sweet or savory?"—then opt for both and arrange them like a gallery exhibit.

3. The Harmonizing Host

Libras make beautiful smoke sessions. They'll:

- Light a candle before lighting the joint
- Play chill-hop or vintage jazz
- Ensure everyone feels emotionally included
- Offer thoughtful compliments to each person before the bowl comes around
- Ask deep questions like, "Do you think our souls chose this life?"—right after laughing about your dog's snore

They blend playfulness with emotional insight. Even their silence is intentional. They're the sign most likely to pause mid-sesh and say, "Let's just appreciate this moment."

Libra's High Tales of Harmony

The Weed & Watercolor Workshop:
One Libra hosted a THC-infused art night where guests painted while high. She had paint palettes, rose petal joints, and a theme: "Self-Love Through Color." Everyone left with a canvas, a cookie, and a newfound appreciation for teal.

The Indecision Spiral:
A Libra once took two gummies and spent the next hour pacing while trying to decide whether to write poetry, do yoga, or clean the kitchen. They ended up reorganizing their bookshelf alphabetically, by color, while reciting love sonnets. It somehow made sense.

The Balanced Relationship Check-In:
High on a mellow hybrid, a Libra initiated a conversation with their partner titled "Are We Emotionally Symmetrical?" They lit sage, poured tea, and discussed the shape of their love. It ended in cuddles and a collaborative playlist.

The Libra Smoke Session
If you're joining a Libra's smoke session, expect:

- Candles, curated aesthetics, and luxurious textures
- The perfect ratio of conversation to introspection
- Multiple snack options presented in matching bowls
- Artistic games or love-themed card pulls
- And lots of back-and-forths before making *any* decision

They want everyone to feel welcome. Everyone to feel heard. And everyone to look *just a little bit better under this lighting.*

Libra Cannabis Compatibility Tips

- **Best Smoking Buddies:** Leo (fun and glam), Gemini (endless convo), Pisces (romantic and reflective)
- **Needs Patience With:** Aries (too blunt), Virgo (too practical), Capricorn (too task-focused)
- **Solo Sessions?** Yes—but they'll make it Instagram-worthy. Libra smokes alone in velvet robes, with jazz playing, while journaling about inner alignment and watching the moon reflect off their teacup.

A Final Puff of Wisdom

Libra reminds us that cannabis isn't just about the sensation—it's about the *experience.* They show us how to blend softness with sophistication, how to make time for beauty, and how to elevate a simple session into something sacred and shared.

Their balance-seeking nature encourages harmony—within and without. When high, Libra teaches us the art of aesthetic presence, emotional grace, and social cohesion. Even when they can't choose between two strains, they still make the choice look beautiful.

So to all the Libra tokers: keep balancing the scales. Keep creating beauty in smoke rings and conversations alike. And if you're still unsure what movie to watch—just pick one. You'll make it magical either way.

Now pass the joint—with both hands—and light a candle for good measure.

Chapter 8: Scorpio – The Intense Infuser

The Alchemist of the Zodiac

Scorpio, the eighth sign of the zodiac, is ruled by Pluto and Mars—forces of transformation, destruction, and raw power. Represented by the Scorpion, Scorpio is the zodiac's deep-sea diver: willing to descend into emotional trenches others fear to acknowledge. This is the sign of secrets, of spiritual rebirth, and of unrelenting emotional authenticity.

When Scorpio gets high, the experience isn't casual—it's **alchemical**. The room darkens, not physically, but emotionally. The air thickens with meaning. Scorpio lights a joint with a question: *What truth have I been avoiding?* Whether it's a solo ritual or a two-person séance, their cannabis journey is ritualistic, intense, and often transformative.

Scorpio at a Glance

- **Element:** Water
- **Modality:** Fixed (emotionally steady, deeply committed)
- **Ruling Planets:** Pluto (transformation), Mars (drive)
- **Keywords:** Passionate, mysterious, powerful, introspective, magnetic
- **Vibe When High:** Penetrating, private, poetic, soul-deep

Scorpios don't smoke to escape—they smoke to investigate. A toke to them is like plunging a torch into their inner cave. They're the ones who do shadow work after one hit, emerge teary-eyed, and declare, *"I forgave my father. Let's do a tarot reading."*

Strains That Match Scorpio's Depth

Scorpio prefers strains that push boundaries—either by intensifying emotion or sharpening focus. They may enjoy heavy indicas for deep internal work or powerful hybrids for vision quests. Some use cannabis as a tool for emotional exorcism, others for erotic amplification.

◈ **Top Strain Picks for Scorpio**

- **Granddaddy Purple:** Deeply relaxing and psychedelic. Perfect for Scorpio's meditative spirals or emotional shedding.
- **Girl Scout Cookies:** Hits hard and brings depth. Good for poetry-writing or emotionally charged conversations.
- **Purple Kush:** Smooth, sedating, and ideal for solo rituals, grief processing, or intimacy with trusted partners.
- **Forbidden Fruit:** Scorpio appreciates the name alone—lush, mysterious, and perfect for taboo-themed journaling.

The Scorpio Cannabis Experience

1. The Sacred Smoker
Scorpio's sessions are **rituals**, not hangouts. Expect:

- Dim lighting, possibly candles
- Incense or oils that smell like earth and forgotten temples
- A playlist featuring ambient trip-hop, rainfall, or cello solos
- A journal opened to a blank page that will later be filled with emotionally coded glyphs no one else understands

They often set an intention before lighting up. That intention? *"Reveal the truth."*

2. The Depth Digger
Scorpio doesn't fear the shadow—they *invite* it. While others giggle or snack, Scorpio may:

- Cry softly with grace
- Write poems to an ex they never sent
- Analyze a dream in three parts (death, transformation, rebirth)
- Enter a trance where they remember past lives as a Babylonian priestess

They are never surface-level. Not even while high. Especially not while high.

3. The Sensual Strategist

Scorpio is also associated with eroticism and magnetism. They may use cannabis to explore:

- Intimate trust rituals
- Sensory expansion in physical touch
- Power dynamics through breath and gaze
- Or just journaling "Do I want them...or do I want to become them?"

Yes, Scorpio asks questions like that while smoking.

Scorpio's High Tales of Transformation

The Shadow Playlist:

One Scorpio curated a 7-song playlist for shadow integration. After a joint and a blackout mask, they meditated to each song while confronting suppressed childhood memories. By track five, they whispered, *"The wound was never mine to carry."* Then got up and made cinnamon tea. Iconic.

The Secret Stash Journal:

Another Scorpio keeps a locked leather notebook only used while high. In it: confessions, psychic visions, forbidden desires, and tarot interpretations of previous lifetimes. They said, *"If I die, burn this book. Or publish it. I haven't decided."*

The Intimate Smoke Pact:

A Scorpio invited a partner to "a shared unraveling." They smoked a deep indica, undressed each other emotionally, and exchanged secrets while blindfolded. Scorpio called it *"high-vulnerability alchemy."* Their partner cried. Scorpio smiled.

The Scorpio Smoke Session

If you're invited to smoke with a Scorpio, be ready:

- To face your inner demons (gently)
- To talk about power, pain, and rebirth
- To be silently stared at while they assess your energy
- To hear things like: *"I trust you. For now."*
- To walk away either transformed or haunted—or both

They're not here for casual vibes. If they let you in, it means something. And if they don't? You won't know they smoked at all.

Scorpio Cannabis Compatibility Tips

- **Best Smoking Buddies:** Pisces (shares emotional depth), Cancer (safe space), Capricorn (brings grounding to Scorpio's intensity)
- **Needs Patience With:** Gemini (too scattered), Sagittarius (too blunt), Leo (too performative)
- **Solo Sessions?** Absolutely. Often. Preferably. Scorpio uses cannabis for solo inner work, energy cleansing, emotional resurrection, and writing mysterious poetry no one will read—but everyone would feel.

A Final Puff of Wisdom

Scorpio shows us the **transformative** potential of cannabis. They teach that getting high isn't always about euphoria—it can be about revelation. Release. Rebirth. Their intensity is not to be feared—it's to be honored. Through smoke and silence, Scorpio reaches into the soul's basement, pulls out the forgotten parts, and breathes life into them.

So to all the Scorpio tokers: keep diving. Keep healing. Keep using cannabis as a torch to light your hidden temples.

Now pass the joint slowly—and tell no one what you saw.

Chapter 9: Sagittarius – The Philosophical Pilgrim

The Cosmic Explorer of the Zodiac

Sagittarius, the ninth sign of the zodiac, is ruled by Jupiter—the planet of expansion, wisdom, travel, and philosophical curiosity. Represented by the Archer (or Centaur), Sagittarius isn't just reaching for the stars—they're aiming to *understand* them. Known for their boundless optimism, infectious laughter, and spiritual wanderlust, Sagittarians are the eternal students of the universe—always seeking new truths, new experiences, and new ways to blow their own minds.

When Sagittarius gets high, it becomes a launchpad—not to escape reality, but to *expand* it. One edible and they're solving existential riddles. One bong hit and they're mapping out the multiverse. Their cannabis highs are wild, euphoric, hilarious, and deeply philosophical—sometimes all at once.

Sagittarius at a Glance

- **Element:** Fire
- **Modality:** Mutable (ever-changing, curious, open-minded)
- **Ruling Planet:** Jupiter
- **Keywords:** Adventurous, idealistic, humorous, spontaneous, philosophical
- **Vibe When High:** Witty, epiphanic, visionary, distracted in the best way

Sagittarians view cannabis the same way they view everything else: as a tool for exploration. Whether they're hiking into a desert canyon with a vape pen or riding a mental zipline through the Akashic Records, they use weed to ask the *big* questions—and sometimes forget the question halfway through because they just saw a cool cloud shaped like a UFO.

Strains That Fuel Sagittarius' Fire

Sagittarius loves highs that offer *lift*, not lethargy. Energizing sativas, mind-opening hybrids, and creative, spiritual strains speak to their essence. They're less interested in sedation and more intrigued by stimulation—especially if it sparks laughter or leads to a mental breakthrough.

⬦ Top Strain Picks for Sagittarius

- **Green Crack:** Bright, cerebral, and fast-paced—perfect for high-speed thought experiments and spontaneous adventures.
- **Durban Poison:** Euphoric and clear-headed, this strain keeps Sagittarius engaged with the cosmos and awake enough to monologue about the meaning of Atlantis.
- **Pineapple Express:** Uplifting and tropical—ideal for Sag's love of good vibes, sunny moods, and stories that start with, *"So there I was, backpacking through..."*
- **LSD:** Introspective, trippy, and revelatory. For Sagittarians who crave metaphysical depth in their highs.

The Sagittarius Cannabis Experience

1. The Wanderer's High

Sagittarius doesn't want to smoke in the same place twice. Their cannabis sessions may occur:

- On a rooftop under the stars
- During a last-minute road trip through forgotten towns
- In the back of a van filled with crystals, guitars, and banana chips
- Or deep in a philosophical group chat that begins with *"What even IS time?"*

They crave movement—even if it's only mental. Sagittarius rarely sits still while high. If their body isn't moving, their mind definitely is.

2. The Cosmic Comedian

Humor is a Sagittarian birthright. Expect:

- Stoned observations like, *"Dogs probably think we're just really tall squirrels."*
- Spirals into metaphysical dad jokes
- Edible-fueled laughter that ends in tears and existential hugs
- Stories from that *one time in Peru* they keep forgetting they already told

They don't just laugh—they *evangelize joy*.

3. The Seeker of Truth

Sagittarius is deeply spiritual. Not in a rigid, ceremonial way—but in a curious, ever-questioning way. When high, they may:

- Rant about reincarnation
- Sketch multidimensional spirit maps
- Pull oracle cards and interpret them through ancient astronaut theory
- Declare they finally "understand string theory" ...then forget it five minutes later

They are walking, blazing question marks—filled with wonder and willing to admit they're often totally wrong (but in a hilarious, lovable way).

Sagittarius's High Tales of Discovery

The Edible Epiphany:

A Sagittarius once took a potent homemade edible and sat down to meditate. Three hours later, they'd written 17 pages of what they claimed was a "channeled future mythos" about post-human dolphins who smoke seagrass and read poetry about black holes. They cried while reading it aloud to their friend's cat.

The Backpack Bong Tour:

Another Sag embarked on a cannabis-themed cross-country road trip, rating dispensaries, meeting spiritual guides, and leaving handwritten notes in bathroom stalls with quotes like, *"Love is a flame. Get high and dance in it."*

The Vision Board Gone Rogue:

Under the influence of a cosmic hybrid, one Sagittarius started a vision board. It spiraled into a mural-sized wall collage of crop circles, dragons, interdimensional portals, and the phrase *"I am my own guru"* in glitter. They still meditate in front of it.

The Sagittarius Smoke Session

If you're invited to smoke with a Sagittarius, prepare for:

- Spontaneous travel plans (even if just to the backyard under a new constellation)
- Wild, unfiltered stories that start funny and end spiritual
- Sudden declarations like, *"We should open a psychedelic retreat on a mountain!"*
- Snack selections based on astrological compatibility ("Taurus snacks with Gemini sauces")
- Conversations that leap from chakras to AI to ancient Mesopotamia in six minutes flat

Sagittarius doesn't get high to unwind—they get high to discover. And maybe jump on a trampoline.

Sagittarius Cannabis Compatibility Tips

- **Best Smoking Buddies:** Aquarius (shares the weird), Aries (loves spontaneity), Leo (adds fire to fire)
- **Needs Patience With:** Virgo (too structured), Cancer (too sensitive for Sag's blunt truths), Scorpio (too intense, not enough giggles)
- **Solo Sessions?** Occasionally. Sagittarius will smoke alone if they're meditating, brainstorming a visionary project, or planning their next spiritual sabbatical to Iceland. But they'd rather have a co-pilot for the journey.

A Final Puff of Wisdom

Sagittarius teaches us that getting high can be an act of joy, philosophy, and *divine restlessness*. They're the ones who remind us to look at the stars, laugh at the absurdity of existence, and never stop asking *why*. Through cannabis, they map new realms—emotional, intellectual, and cosmic.

They don't use weed to escape life. They use it to find more of it.

So to all the Sagittarius tokers: keep questing. Keep expanding. Keep lighting the joint of truth and passing it to the universe.

Now eat the gummy, pack the bag, and let's find out what's *really* at the edge of the map.

Chapter 10: Capricorn – The High Achiever

The Executive of the Zodiac

Capricorn, the tenth sign of the zodiac, is ruled by Saturn—the planet of time, discipline, legacy, and structure. Represented by the Sea Goat, Capricorn climbs steadily toward the summit of any ambition, armed with focus, resilience, and a planner so detailed it has contingency plans for its contingency plans.

When Capricorn gets high, it's not to waste time—it's to *use* it. Every puff has purpose. Every edible is microdosed. Their cannabis use is strategic, measured, and frequently tied to goal-setting, task completion, or stress decompression. If a Capricorn is smoking, they've earned it—and they'll still check their emails afterward.

Capricorn at a Glance

- **Element:** Earth
- **Modality:** Cardinal (initiates systems and structures)
- **Ruling Planet:** Saturn
- **Keywords:** Ambitious, practical, self-disciplined, goal-oriented, resourceful
- **Vibe When High:** Calm, structured, forward-thinking, ironically hilarious

Capricorns aren't stoners—they're **cannabis strategists**. They may not smoke often, but when they do, it's either to engineer a five-year plan or reward themselves after finishing one. They don't chase highs—they manage them like they manage everything else: efficiently.

Strains That Sharpen Capricorn's Grind

Capricorns prefer strains that keep them clear, grounded, and productive. They're cautious with anything too intense or disorienting and often choose strains that assist with stress relief, deep focus, or quiet reflection. Even when they indulge, they prefer cannabis that respects their time.

◈ Top Strain Picks for Capricorn

- **Jack Herer:** A cerebral, energizing sativa that boosts productivity and clarity. Perfect for Capricorn's early-morning strategy sessions.
- **Blue Dream:** Reliable and functional—this balanced hybrid allows Capricorn to brainstorm without becoming foggy.
- **Afghan Kush:** For deep relaxation after a long day of climbing metaphorical mountains.
- **Super Lemon Haze:** A citrusy, energizing pick-me-up for goal mapping, vision boards, or spreadsheets with flair.

The Capricorn Cannabis Experience

1. The Productive Puff
Capricorn's high comes with a to-do list. They may:

- Use cannabis to help complete menial tasks
- Brainstorm new business models
- Edit a manuscript or build a content calendar
- Create a financial forecast while snacking on infused dark chocolate

They're the person who finishes your joint and then asks, *"Have you updated your budget for Q4?"*

2. The Time-Conscious Toker
Every moment has value to Capricorn. If they light up, they:

- Set timers
- Pre-roll their joints with maximum efficiency
- Choose doses based on whether they have deadlines the next morning
- May *schedule* their high in their planner between "client meeting" and "laundry"

Don't take it personally. Their time management is how they survive capitalism.

3. The Reward Ritualist

Capricorns may use cannabis as a personal ritual after achieving something. Expect:

- A victory blunt after closing a contract
- A meditative edible post-launch
- A rare but luxurious THC bath bomb used only after meeting every milestone for the quarter

They may say, *"I can't relax until the job is done."* Then take the deepest, most satisfying inhale you've ever witnessed.

Capricorn's High Tales of Hustle

The Edible Entrepreneur:
One Capricorn microdosed edibles to help them think outside the box for their startup pitch deck. They reorganized their entire brand in four hours, then went on to secure funding—stoned, steady, and spectacular.

The High Planner Hack:
Another Cap turned a late-night smoke session into a time management experiment. They color-coded their planner by THC strength, tracked focus cycles, and created a flowchart titled: "Optimal Cannabis States for Creative Output." It now lives on a productivity subreddit.

The Capricorn Canna-Coach:
A Capricorn who rarely smoked decided to try journaling while high. The results? A 25-page self-improvement workbook titled *"Discipline, Elevated."* It included charts, timelines, and motivational mantras. They made it available for download—and yes, they charged for it.

The Capricorn Smoke Session
If you're lucky enough to share a session with a Capricorn:

- Don't be surprised if they show up with a notepad
- They'll likely ask what the strain is, its effects, and when it was harvested
- The vibe will be calm, quiet, and intentional
- They may steer the conversation toward investments, projects, or "legacy planning"
- Even if they're giggling, they're still tracking how many hits they've taken

It's not that they can't let go. They just want to let go *intelligently.*

Capricorn Cannabis Compatibility Tips

- **Best Smoking Buddies:** Virgo (organized fun), Taurus (grounded luxury), Scorpio (intensity + mutual respect)
- **Needs Patience With:** Sagittarius (too chaotic), Gemini (too scattered), Pisces (too dreamy for Cap's liking)
- **Solo Sessions?** Preferred. Capricorn enjoys private, structured highs where they can analyze, decompress, or refine a project in peace—possibly while sipping herbal tea and running a scented oil diffuser.

A Final Puff of Wisdom

Capricorn teaches us that cannabis doesn't have to mean losing control—it can mean gaining *clarity*. They remind us that structure can co-exist with elevation, that laughter doesn't mean laziness, and that a little weed might just be the boost your business plan needs.

So to all the Capricorn tokers: keep climbing. Keep building. Keep lighting up not just for escape—but for evolution.

Now spark the joint, open the spreadsheet, and let's turn dreams into deadlines.

Chapter 11: Aquarius – The Eccentric Innovator

The Visionary of the Zodiac

Aquarius, the eleventh sign of the zodiac, is ruled by Uranus—the planet of innovation, rebellion, and sudden insight. Represented by the Water Bearer, Aquarius pours knowledge into the world, often ahead of its time, sometimes to its own social peril. Detached, experimental, and deeply idealistic, Aquarians are the mad scientists of the astrological world—dreaming of better futures, then figuring out how to engineer them from the garage.

When Aquarius gets high, it's not just recreational—it's *revolutionary.* This is the zodiac's inventor, the pot-smoking philosopher, the cannabis chemist who creates new rituals no one's ever tried. They're building infused kombucha in the closet and brushing their teeth with weed-flavored toothpaste while designing a commune in the cloud.

Aquarius at a Glance

- **Element:** Air
- **Modality:** Fixed (stubborn, focused, radical thinker)
- **Ruling Planet:** Uranus
- **Keywords:** Innovative, eccentric, rebellious, intellectual, futuristic
- **Vibe When High:** Detached, cosmic, absurdly clever, comfortably weird

Aquarians aren't your typical tokers. They're *experimenters.* One hit and they're discussing transhumanism. Two hits and they're wondering if the joint is a metaphor for society. Three hits and they're halfway into a DIY project to turn their couch into a hovercraft.

Strains That Light Aquarius's Circuit Board

Aquarius doesn't just look for "good weed"—they look for *experimental experiences.* Whether it's rare terpenes, space-themed strains, or custom-grow blends, they want something different. They enjoy mental stimulation, introspection, and wild thought chains that end in mind-mapping their own cult (sorry—*intentional community*).

◈ **Top Strain Picks for Aquarius**

- **Space Queen:** Euphoric and mentally uplifting—perfect for launching Aquarian theories into hyperspace.
- **Chocolope:** A creative, focused sativa for diving into abstract concepts or building weird tech on weed.
- **Cannabis Caviar (moon rocks):** High potency, high uniqueness—Aquarius is fascinated by its layered design.
- **Lamb's Bread:** For ethical clarity and Bob Marley-esque peace-building vibes. Great for visionary group chats.

The Aquarius Cannabis Experience

1. The Tinkering Toker

Aquarius treats cannabis like a science experiment. You'll find them:

- Mixing their own topicals in beakers
- Trying out cannabis-infused toothpaste, breath strips, or herbal shampoos
- Vaping through obscure tech setups that involve lasers, sound waves, or Bluetooth
- Creating spreadsheets titled *"Potency to Creativity Ratios – Cross-Strain Analysis"*

They don't just get high—they *engineer* the high.

2. The Social Rebel

Aquarians often smoke in groups, but not for basic bonding—they want to:

- Start a utopian think tank
- Discuss surveillance ethics while passing a joint
- Plan an off-grid village with a communal edible bakery
- Host TED-style high talks titled: *"Rewiring the Matrix: The Role of THC in Future Consciousness"*

They're not trying to be weird. They *are* weird. And proud of it.

3. The Detached Dreamer

Aquarius has emotions—but they process them through metaphors, algorithms, and future timelines. When high, they might:

- Build a robot to process their feelings
- Write a zine titled *"Heartbreak in the Age of AI"*
- Cry during a sci-fi anime, then immediately research quantum love theory
- Get very into astrology—but only the kind with infographics and obscure planets like Eris

Aquarius's High Tales of Innovation

The THC Toothpaste Formula:
One Aquarius mixed mint oil, decarboxylated THC, and activated charcoal to create "Dentabuzz"—an energizing morning brushing ritual. They swore it made them smarter. Side effects included giggling through Zoom meetings and frequent dental conversations at parties.

The Edible Utopia Blueprint:
High on moon rocks and oat milk, an Aquarian wrote a 23-page proposal for a floating commune powered by hemp batteries and governed by consensus-based rituals. It included a cannabis-infused bartering system, crop-sharing incentives, and a weekly stargazing ceremony. They emailed it to Elon Musk. No response (yet).

The Anti-Capitalist Smoke Circle:
During a full moon, an Aquarius invited friends to a clothing-optional bonfire where they smoked Blue Dream and shredded expired student loan bills. Between bowls, they debated the blockchain's role in art equity. Someone brought a laser harp. It was a success.

The Aquarius Smoke Session
Join an Aquarius smoke session and expect:

- Experimental gear, like bongs made from lab glass or 3D printers
- Philosophical questions like, *"What if the universe is high on us?"*
- Deep silences followed by bursts of insight
- Playlists with titles like *"Post-Human Chillwave Vibes"*
- Snacks you've never seen before (freeze-dried edamame or edible glitter gum)

They'll challenge your assumptions, tweak the rules of the session, and possibly reinvent cannabis etiquette by accident.

Aquarius Cannabis Compatibility Tips

- **Best Smoking Buddies:** Sagittarius (equally wild ideas), Libra (loves cerebral discussion), Gemini (curious and fast-paced)
- **Needs Patience With:** Taurus (too rigid), Cancer (too emotional), Capricorn (too structured)
- **Solo Sessions?** Frequently. Aquarius values alone time to think, prototype, or write speculative fiction in a blanket fort with a vape pen and a whiteboard.

A Final Puff of Wisdom

Aquarius shows us that cannabis isn't just a plant—it's a **portal.** A strange, beautiful substance that unlocks thought patterns, future visions, and emotional inventions. Their highs are never boring, never predictable, and always a little revolutionary.

They remind us that it's okay to be strange, to think big, and to break all the old rules—even when it comes to how you toke.

So to all the Aquarian tokers: keep experimenting. Keep dreaming weird. Keep turning smoke into blueprints for better worlds.

Now pack the moon rock, dim the lights, and ask yourself—what would aliens do?

Chapter 12: Pisces – The Dreamy Dabbler

The Mystic of the Zodiac

Pisces, the twelfth and final sign of the zodiac, is ruled by Neptune—the planet of dreams, illusions, transcendence, and spirituality. Represented by two fish swimming in opposite directions, Pisces lives between worlds: part earth, part ocean, part stardust. They are the empaths, the artists, the intuitive dreamers who feel what others deny, who imagine what others forget.

When Pisces gets high, reality becomes *optional*. A puff for a Pisces is an invitation to drift. Their cannabis experience isn't recreational—it's a foggy ferry ride to the edge of the soul. They light up not just to relax, but to *merge*—with art, with others, with the cosmic flow itself.

Pisces at a Glance

- **Element:** Water
- **Modality:** Mutable (fluid, flexible, perceptive)
- **Ruling Planet:** Neptune
- **Keywords:** Imaginative, emotional, spiritual, compassionate, whimsical
- **Vibe When High:** Soft-focus, artistic, sentimental, surreal

Pisces doesn't "get high"—they *become* the high. Their sessions are often more ethereal than euphoric. You'll find them blending incense, stargazing under soft blankets, or whispering affirmations into a rose quartz pipe.

Strains That Support Pisces' Softened Reality

Pisces gravitates toward strains that inspire creativity, emotional insight, and peace. Gentle hybrids, calming indicas, or strains known for deep, dreamlike effects are their go-to choices. They want to feel safe in the fog, not lost in it.

◈ Top Strain Picks for Pisces

- **Blueberry:** Soothing and blissful—perfect for late-night poetry or cuddling with an oracle deck.
- **Northern Lights:** Euphoric, sleepy, and mystical. Pisces uses it to stargaze or drift into guided meditations.
- **Lavender Kush:** Floral, calming, and sensory-rich. Enhances Pisces' need for aesthetic intoxication.
- **Skywalker OG:** A floating, astral strain for leaving the body gently while still keeping a soul-string tethered.

The Pisces Cannabis Experience

1. The Ambient Artist

Pisces uses cannabis as an *artistic enhancer*. Expect:

- High-fueled painting with soft synths in the background
- Freestyle singing into a crystal-studded vape
- Journal entries that read like dream-sequences
- Sketchbooks filled with cosmic maps, mermaid sigils, or cryptic water poems

They create not for recognition, but for release.

2. The Sentimental Stoner

Pisces gets *emotional* while high. You might find them:

- Crying during a playlist they made for a pet that died six years ago
- Hugging a friend and whispering, "You're the reason I believe in light"
- Watching animated films and saying things like, *"This jellyfish speaks to my soul"*

They don't fight the current of their feelings—they *float* in it.

3. The Astral Traveler

Pisces excels at altered states. With the right strain and setting, they may:

- Meditate into the dreamworld
- Fall asleep mid-conversation and astrally visit your subconscious
- Hear whispers of spirit guides who smell like cannabis smoke and lavender
- Wake up and declare, *"I was a phoenix in another life and I remember the fire."*

They're not kidding. Pisces doesn't make it up—they channel it.

Pisces' High Tales of Transcendence

The Celestial Playlist Curation:
One Pisces claimed their edible kicked in just as a comet passed overhead. They immediately created a playlist called *"Starlight Cry Sessions"* and cried to track three titled *"Moonlight in My Lungs."* They later added it to a public folder titled *"Audio for Astral Travel."*

The Dream Doodle Diary:
Another Pisces spent three hours drawing visions they had while meditating on an indica high. The art included a floating fish queen, a coral cathedral, and a jellyfish playing a harp. When asked what it meant, they said: *"It's a soul-memory. Not everything needs to be understood."*

The Smoke and Soak Ritual:
Every Sunday, one Pisces smokes Lavender Kush, runs a ritual bath with rose petals, ocean sounds, and moonwater, then writes affirmations on steamed mirrors. Their sacred mantra: *"I forgive the ocean for being too much, because I am too much and that's divine."*

The Pisces Smoke Session

Smoking with a Pisces is a portal. Be ready for:

- Candlelit circles with crystals and mood lighting
- Snack tables with seaweed chips, pastel macarons, and something shaped like a moon
- Conversations that start with astrology and end with dream theory
- Fluffy robes, fuzzy socks, and ambient playlists titled *"Liminal Drift"*

Pisces will likely forget to pass the joint because they're busy staring into a lava lamp and having a past-life memory.

Pisces Cannabis Compatibility Tips

- **Best Smoking Buddies:** Scorpio (shared depth), Cancer (mutual nurturing), Aquarius (shares a love of weird)
- **Needs Patience With:** Aries (too brash), Gemini (too fast), Virgo (too grounded)
- **Solo Sessions?** Frequently. Pisces uses solo highs for dream journaling, emotional cleansing, poetry writing, and downloading intuitive messages from the cosmos.

A Final Puff of Wisdom

Pisces teaches us that cannabis isn't just about feeling good—it's about **feeling *everything*.** Through soft highs and spiritual fog, they remind us of the magic of surrender. Their dreamy, emotional, and cosmic lens reveals that cannabis can be a bridge between the known and the numinous.

So to all the Pisces tokers: keep drifting. Keep feeling. Keep weaving smoke into stardust and painting the sky with your sighs.

Now cue the ambient stargaze playlist, light a rose-scented joint, and float into the infinite with open arms.

Chapter 13: Zodiac Strain Pairings – The Ultimate Cheat Sheet

The Stars Have Spoken—And They Brought Weed

Let's be honest—choosing a cannabis strain can feel as overwhelming as picking a Netflix show after three edibles. But what if the cosmos could make the decision for you? What if your zodiac sign came with its own flavor profile, energetic rhythm, and high-vibe match made in herb heaven?

Welcome to the *Zodiac Strain Pairings Cheat Sheet*, where the stars roll the joints, the signs light the flame, and the universe passes the blunt (clockwise, please—respect the ritual). Whether you're a philosophical Sagittarius or a high-maintenance Leo, we've paired each sign with its ideal cannabis strains—and added a wink of humor to help you laugh through the haze.

Grab your grinder. This one's written in the leaves *and* the stars.

◇ Aries – The Fiery Initiator

Strain Match: Green Crack

Why: Because Aries wakes up at 7 a.m. ready to climb a mountain, punch the sky, and start three new projects before breakfast. Green Crack delivers that hyper-zing energy to match Aries' impulsive charge—and fuels their infamous snack raids.

Bonus Pairing: Trainwreck – when they want to argue with Siri and win.

◈ **Taurus – The Velvet Lounge Lizard**

Strain Match: Northern Lights

Why: Taurus doesn't *smoke weed*—they *luxuriate* in it. Northern Lights offers that soft, heavy blanket of calm they crave while lounging in silk pajamas, with a charcuterie board and lo-fi jazz playing.

Bonus Pairing: Bubba Kush – for uninterrupted naps between bites of truffle popcorn.

◈ **Gemini – The Chatty Cloud Surfer**

Strain Match: Chocolope

Why: Gemini needs a strain that can keep up with their 47 simultaneous thoughts. Chocolope offers cerebral stimulation without making them forget how to speak—or why they were speaking in the first place.

Bonus Pairing: Jack Herer – because Geminis deserve a strain as high-functioning and hyper as they are.

◈ Cancer – The Sentimental Smoke Whisperer

Strain Match: Blueberry

Why: Cancers get high and start rewatching home videos, crying over old text messages, and texting their ex with, *"I forgive you but I'm still emotionally scarred."* Blueberry calms the tides and wraps them in a comforting haze.

Bonus Pairing: Granddaddy Purple – for those full moon feels and bathtub confessionals.

◈ Leo – The Regal Smoker of Center Stage

Strain Match: Pineapple Express

Why: Leos want a strain that shines as bright as they do. Pineapple Express is flavorful, energetic, and cinematic—just like Leo's ideal selfie lighting. Bonus: it enhances karaoke confidence.

Bonus Pairing: Sunset Sherbet – because Leos deserve luxury with sparkle.

◈ Virgo – The Analytical Inhaler

Strain Match: Harlequin (High-CBD)

Why: Virgos want functional highs that won't mess up their spreadsheets. Harlequin's CBD-rich calm helps them relax without spiraling into existential dread about whether the kitchen sponge has germs.

Bonus Pairing: Super Lemon Haze – to clean the entire apartment *and* reorganize their emotional life.

◈ Libra – The Aesthetic Smoke Curator

Strain Match: Wedding Cake

Why: Libras smoke for balance, beauty, and Instagrammable vibes. Wedding Cake offers a sweet, euphoric high perfect for deep conversations and soft lighting. Bonus points if the joint is wrapped in rose petals.

Bonus Pairing: Gelato – smooth, elegant, and indecisive-friendly.

◈ Scorpio – The Intense Infuser of Secrets

Strain Match: LSD

Why: Scorpio doesn't want a buzz—they want a *transformation*. LSD delivers the metaphysical punch they crave, sending them into poetic journaling, shadow work, and suspicious eye contact with strangers.

Bonus Pairing: Death Star – because subtlety isn't in their smoke vocabulary.

◈ Sagittarius – The Wandering Weed Philosopher

Strain Match: Durban Poison

Why: Sag needs a high that fuels movement, thought, and impulsive road trips. Durban Poison offers bright mental clarity, energy, and an urge to explain Atlantis over tacos.

Bonus Pairing: Maui Wowie – for high-vibe, beach-blazing enlightenment.

◈ Capricorn – The Strategic Smoker

Strain Match: Jack Herer

Why: Capricorns don't smoke to giggle—they smoke to *execute*. Jack Herer brings productivity, focus, and just enough creative fire to blueprint a legacy... then review the budget.

Bonus Pairing: Afghan Kush – as a reward after they've finished conquering the world.

◈ Aquarius – The Cosmic Contrarian

Strain Match: Space Queen

Why: Aquarians aren't here for your basic hybrid. Space Queen delivers a trippy, out-there experience that aligns with their inner alien and fuels their latest idea for hemp-powered hover bikes.

Bonus Pairing: Moon Rocks – high as hell, weird as hell, *perfect*.

◈ Pisces – The Dreamboat Dabber

Strain Match: Lavender Kush

Why: Pisces needs softness, serenity, and something that enhances their soul-melting playlists. Lavender Kush gives them the dreamy float they desire—ideal for sketching mermaid prophecies at 3 a.m.

Bonus Pairing: Skywalker OG – because why *not* astral project during a snack break?

Cosmic Bonus: Sun, Moon, and Rising Smoke Strategy

- **Sun Sign:** Your go-to strain for personality alignment
- **Moon Sign:** Your emotional support strain
- **Rising Sign:** Your social session vibe strain

Example:

If you're a Taurus Sun, Cancer Moon, and Gemini Rising:
→ Smoke Bubba Kush to relax, Blueberry when emotional, and Chocolope when you're trying to make five new friends in one hour.

Closing Puff of Wisdom

There's no *wrong* way to match your cannabis to your zodiac—only *more cosmic* ways. Whether you're choosing based on mood, moon, or just your craving for citrus, let the stars guide your stash. Laugh a little, light a lot (responsibly), and trust your inner sign to know what it needs.

Now roll your star sign, spark your rising, and inhale like your moon depends on it.

Chapter 14: Celebrity Sessions – Imaginary Smoke Circles of the Stars

Lights, Camera, Inhale.

What if the stars—both astrological *and* Hollywood—got together to pass the peace pipe? Imagine a world where your favorite celebrities gathered by zodiac sign, rolled their ideal strains, and created sessions so legendary they'd be whispered about in velvet lounges for decades.

This chapter doesn't list who *actually* smokes cannabis. This is fantasy. Satire. A star-struck smoke-dream of what might happen if Beyoncé brought a blunt to a Libra picnic, or if Keanu Reeves shared a spiritual edible with Aquarians while decoding time.

Grab your popcorn (infused, obviously). These are **celebrity smoke circles by sign**—fictional, hilarious, and written in the fog of imagination.

◈ Aries – The Chaos Blaze Squad

Celebrity Session: Lady Gaga, Robert Downey Jr., and Russell Crowe

Setting: A rooftop dojo with punching bags, a boom box, and zero chill.

Strain of Choice: Trainwreck + Red Bull + reckless optimism.

Highlights:

- Gaga starts freestyling in six accents.
- RDJ invents a THC-fueled Iron Man upgrade.
- Russell tries to arm-wrestle the moon.
- All three decide to start a band. They forget by sunrise.

◈ Taurus – The Luxe Lounge Circle

Celebrity Session: Adele, David Beckham, and Gal Gadot

Setting: A velvet Moroccan tent filled with plush pillows, slow jazz, and snacks curated by Michelin-star chefs.

Strain of Choice: Northern Lights with edible truffles and rosé.

Highlights:

- Adele laughs herself into a singing fit and turns it into a mini-concert.
- Beckham adjusts the lighting until it's perfect for selfies.
- Gal Gadot recites poetry in four languages while moisturizing.
- Nobody leaves for six hours. And nobody wants to.

⬦ Gemini – The Talkative Toke Collective

Celebrity Session: Kanye West, Tom Holland, and Helena Bonham Carter

Setting: An LED-lit treehouse with microphones, tarot cards, and three podcast mics that are definitely recording.

Strain of Choice: Chocolope and whatever sativa was invented last week.

Highlights:

- Tom flips upside down mid-story just to make a point.
- Helena reads tea leaves in a British accent even though they're smoking.
- Kanye turns the session into a TED Talk about vibration consciousness.
- The joint goes missing halfway through because everyone forgot to pass it.

◈ **Cancer – The Feel-Your-Feels Circle**

Celebrity Session: Lana Del Rey, Selena Gomez, and Chris Pratt

Setting: A blanket fort shaped like a seashell with candlelight, incense, and soft whale noises.

Strain of Choice: Blueberry with chamomile tea and emotional snacks.

Highlights:

- Lana journals by moonlight while crying beautifully.
- Selena leads a group cuddle and forgiveness ritual.
- Chris brings homemade brownies that taste like childhood.
- Everyone leaves more healed than high.

◈ Leo – The Spotlight Smoke Soirée

Celebrity Session: Beyoncé, Ryan Reynolds, and Zendaya

Setting: A gold-trimmed rooftop with fireworks, mirrors, and a fan that makes your hair look perfect in slow-mo.

Strain of Choice: Pineapple Express with glittery pre-rolls.

Highlights:

- Beyoncé rolls the joint with one hand while giving a motivational speech.
- Ryan tells jokes until the moon laughs.
- Zendaya struts in slow motion for no reason and wins the session.
- Paparazzi try to crash but get hugged into submission.

◈ Virgo – The Herbalist Harmony Circle

Celebrity Session: Emma Watson, Keanu Reeves, and Timothée Chalamet

Setting: An eco-conscious greenhouse with herbal charts, wellness elixirs, and color-coded rolling trays.

Strain of Choice: Harlequin + CBD-infused cucumber water.

Highlights:

- Emma gives a speech on cannabis history and safe dosing.
- Keanu stares into a crystal and gently says, *"We are all the leaf."*
- Timothée alphabetizes the snacks.
- Nobody gets too high, but everyone leaves more aligned.

◈ Libra – The Aesthetic Puff Party

Celebrity Session: Doja Cat, Harry Styles, and Blake Lively

Setting: A lakeside picnic with flower crowns, rose quartz bowls, and a fashion photographer lurking in the bushes.

Strain of Choice: Wedding Cake and champagne-kissed vape pens.

Highlights:

- Doja designs a zodiac-themed outfit mid-high.
- Harry Styles paints everyone's aura in watercolor.
- Blake brings matching edible cupcakes and legal disclaimers.
- The entire event trends as #SmokeSymmetry2025.

◈ Scorpio – The Smoke-and-Shadow Coven

Celebrity Session: Billie Eilish, Jared Leto, and Angelina Jolie

Setting: A candlelit circle on an abandoned stage where mirrors face mirrors.

Strain of Choice: LSD (the strain) and whispered secrets.

Highlights:

- Billie floats during a spoken word confession.
- Jared declares himself immortal and vanishes for 10 minutes.
- Angelina summons a memory from 2006 and forgives it in Latin.
- No one saw them arrive. No one saw them leave.

◈ Sagittarius – The Cosmic Comedy Caravan

Celebrity Session: Snoop Dogg, Jennifer Lawrence, and Jason Momoa

Setting: A bonfire on a beach with surfboards, hammocks, and constellation games.

Strain of Choice: Durban Poison and Maui Wowie trail mix.

Highlights:

- J-Law accidentally eats four edibles and gives a TED Talk on pizza.
- Snoop narrates the night in rhymes while feeding everyone.
- Momoa tries to ride the moon and almost succeeds.
- They all end up skinny-dipping and laughing at clouds.

◈ Capricorn – The Strategic Smoke Syndicate

Celebrity Session: Michelle Obama, Denzel Washington, and Benedict Cumberbatch

Setting: A candlelit library with leather chairs, legacy maps, and achievement incense.

Strain of Choice: Jack Herer followed by power naps.

Highlights:

- Michelle outlines her next book, three chapters deep, mid-hit.
- Denzel leads a motivational vision board workshop.
- Benedict creates a Sherlock-themed THC tea pairing.
- Every goal on the dream board gets checked off—*twice*.

✧ Aquarius – The Galactic Vibe Pod

Celebrity Session: Grimes, Donald Glover, and Keanu Reeves (again—he belongs here too)

Setting: A neon-lit dome with projection-mapped walls, 3D-printed pipes, and ambient alien house music.

Strain of Choice: Space Queen + terpene experiments.

Highlights:

- Grimes floats in a VR suit and draws a cyber-baby.
- Donald freestyles about Saturn's rings.
- Keanu programs a compassionate AI while microdosing truth.
- The entire session is streamed to another galaxy.

◈ Pisces – The Mystic Dream Drift

Celebrity Session: Rihanna, Tim Burton, and Florence Welch

Setting: A starlit garden by a koi pond with fog machines, moonlight, and soft harp loops.

Strain of Choice: Lavender Kush, followed by guided crystal healing.

Highlights:

- Rihanna sings lullabies into the clouds.
- Florence dances barefoot while whispering astrology secrets.
- Tim sketches stoned koi fish and cries about their symbolism.
- Everyone swears they briefly became the sky.

Final Puff: Who Would You Smoke With?

In the dream lounge of astrology and fame, there's a circle for everyone. Whether you vibe with Capricorn's planners or Pisces' dreamscapes, these fictional sessions remind us: cannabis creates connection, storytelling, and laughter—even among stars.

Now light up your imagination, roll a fantasy blunt, and ask yourself—who's in *your* smoke circle?

Chapter 15: Celestial Strain Pairings for Social Events

When Stars Align, So Should the Strains

You've gathered your zodiac crew. The snacks are out. The lighters are charged. But one question lingers in the cosmic air: *What are we smoking tonight?*

Hosting an astrologically aligned smoke circle isn't just about picking the strongest strain—it's about **harmony**. Each sign brings a different energy to the sesh: some want to talk philosophy, others just want to vibe. Some are down to roll, others forgot what planet they're on. A balanced circle means honoring these different dynamics—and matching the right strains to uplift, soothe, or center the cosmic chaos.

Welcome to the art of celestial strain pairings for social events. Whether you're hosting a lunar picnic, a birthday blaze-off, or a retrograde recovery party, this guide will help you craft a cannabis experience that's written in the stars.

Understanding the Social Astrology Matrix

Before we get to the strains, let's break down how each zodiac group contributes to the vibe:

- **Fire Signs (Aries, Leo, Sagittarius):** Bring energy, jokes, volume, and boldness. Need uplifting, adventurous strains.
- **Earth Signs (Taurus, Virgo, Capricorn):** Ground the group, manage details, ensure snacks and cleanup. Prefer calming, functional strains.
- **Air Signs (Gemini, Libra, Aquarius):** Spark conversation, creativity, and unexpected games. Best with cerebral, social strains.
- **Water Signs (Cancer, Scorpio, Pisces):** Provide emotional depth, spiritual vibes, and intuitive music selection. Love dreamy, euphoric highs.

A successful smoke circle balances these four elements like a living ritual: fire to initiate, earth to stabilize, air to expand, and water to connect.

Celestial Smoke Circle Format: 4-Step Blueprint

1. **Astrological Theme:** Choose a reason to gather—New Moon, full moon, a birthday, retrograde, or even just "Venus entered Leo and we need to slay."
2. **Guest Alignment:** Know who's coming and what signs they bring. Are you balancing all four elements, or is this a wild fire-sign-heavy situation?
3. **Strain Strategy:** Select 2–3 strains that complement or balance the signs in the room.
4. **Set the Scene:** Music, lighting, food, and accessories all matter. Make the environment match the signs and strains for maximum synchronicity.

Event Examples + Ideal Strain Pairings

◈ 1. Full Moon Healing Circle (Water Energy)
Guest Vibe: Cancer, Pisces, Scorpio, Taurus
Mood: Soft, sacred, emotional release
Ideal Strains:

- *Blueberry* – Gentle, euphoric, nurturing
- *Granddaddy Purple* – Deeply relaxing, emotionally grounding
- *Lavender Kush* – Floral, tranquil, perfect for meditation
  Add Ons: Crystals, moon water, slow music, soft blankets, journaling prompts

◈ 2. New Moon Manifestation Party (Fire + Air Energy)
Guest Vibe: Aries, Leo, Sagittarius, Gemini
Mood: Energetic, expressive, vision-focused
Ideal Strains:

- *Durban Poison* – Bright, talkative, focused
- *Green Crack* – Activating, idea-generating
- *Pineapple Express* – Uplifting and cinematic
  Add Ons: Vision boards, incense, open mic sharing, sparkly decor

◈ **3. Birthday Bash by Sign (Zodiac-Specific Theme)**
Guest Vibe: Centered on one sign and their best friend signs
Mood: Personalized to birthday sign
Example – Libra Birthday
Strains:

- *Wedding Cake* – Balanced, sweet, aesthetic
- *Gelato* – Smooth social vibes
- *Jack Herer* – For those friends who won't shut up

Add Ons: Fancy snacks, music curation, curated gift bags with rolling papers or crystals aligned with that sign

◈ **4. Retrograde Recovery Lounge (Earth Energy)**
Guest Vibe: Virgo, Capricorn, Aquarius, Cancer
Mood: Slow, grounding, supportive
Ideal Strains:

- *Harlequin* – High-CBD clarity
- *Afghan Kush* – Deep rest and chill
- *ACDC* – Functional, gentle, grounding
  Add Ons: Weighted blankets, tea, nonverbal games, relaxing scents like sandalwood or sage

◈ 5. Cosmic Creativity Night (Air + Water Blend)

Guest Vibe: Pisces, Libra, Gemini, Aquarius
Mood: Artistic, dreamy, whimsical
Ideal Strains:

- *Chocolope* – Thought-provoking and giggly
- *Skywalker OG* – Cosmic, floaty
- *Space Queen* – Euphoric and slightly weird
  Add Ons: Paint stations, poetry readings, ambient lighting, synthwave playlists

◈ 6. Sacred Solo Smoke Ceremony (For All Signs)

Guest Vibe: Just you and the universe
Mood: Self-reflection, energy clearing, intention setting
Ideal Strains Based on Sun Sign:

- **Aries:** Jack Herer – Focused but fiery
- **Taurus:** Bubba Kush – Calming and comforting
- **Gemini:** Lemon Haze – Light and energizing
- **Cancer:** Northern Lights – Gentle emotional release
- **Leo:** Purple Punch – Relaxed but dramatic
- **Virgo:** ACDC – Clear and manageable
- **Libra:** Gelato – Balanced and social
- **Scorpio:** LSD – Introspective and potent
- **Sagittarius:** Maui Wowie – Wanderlust in a bowl
- **Capricorn:** Afghan Kush – Efficient and grounding
- **Aquarius:** Moon Rocks – Out-of-this-world
- **Pisces:** Lavender Kush – Soft and dreamy

Add Ons: A personal altar, mirror rituals, candle gazing, or meditation music

Signs & Their Ideal Roles in the Circle

Zodiac Sign	Best Smoke Circle Role
Aries	Energy starter & hype wizard
Taurus	Snack coordinator & vibe guardian
Gemini	Conversation host & joke supplier
Cancer	Emotional support & playlist alchemist
Leo	Photographer & group organizer
Virgo	Grinder guardian & dose manager
Libra	Aesthetic curator & harmony referee
Scorpio	Joint roller & shadow guide
Sagittarius	Storyteller & rule-breaker
Capricorn	Timer keeper & cleanup hero
Aquarius	Game master & tech assistant
Pisces	Spiritual guide & nap facilitator

Celestial Pairing Matrix – 3 Sign Sample Circles

◈ *The Firestorm Trio* **(Aries, Leo, Sagittarius)**
Strains: Green Crack, Pineapple Express
Activities: Dance battle, improv games, spontaneous karaoke

◈ *The Water Wavelength* **(Cancer, Scorpio, Pisces)**
Strains: Blueberry, Lavender Kush
Activities: Guided meditation, silent journaling, tea and tarot

◈ *The Airwave Party* **(Gemini, Libra, Aquarius)**
Strains: Chocolope, Jack Herer
Activities: Rolling competition, truth-or-dare, group storytelling

Final Puff: Let the Stars Choose the Strains

When you plan your next session, remember: cannabis isn't one-size-fits-all. And neither are your guests. By respecting each sign's energy—and choosing strains that create balance—you're not just smoking. You're building *ritual*. You're weaving a moment of connection, laughter, and starlit synchronicity.

So next time someone asks what strain to roll, tell them—"Let's ask the stars."

Chapter 16: Planetary Retrogrades & Cannabis Remedies

When the Planets Backpedal, You Light Up

There's a collective sigh in the air—and no, it's not just the exhale of a smoke circle. It's Mercury retrograde again, and everything from text messages to travel plans seems to spiral into cosmic chaos. But Mercury isn't the only celestial body that throws shade on your routine. Every planet retrogrades, and each one hits a different part of your soul like a misfired edible.

But fear not: for every planetary retrograde, there is a cannabis remedy. The right strain can help you not only survive these backward planetary drags—but *thrive* through them.

This chapter is your **astro-herbal first aid kit**, packed with wisdom, weed, and cosmic clarity. Whether it's your GPS glitching mid-journey or your ex sliding into your DMs at 3 a.m., we've got you covered—with flower, vape, tincture, or edible.

Understanding Retrograde Energy: Why You Feel Like You're in a Funhouse

When a planet goes retrograde, it appears to move backward in the sky from our perspective on Earth. In astrology, retrogrades symbolize periods of **review, recalibration, reflection, and resets.** They're meant to slow us down—but modern life doesn't like to pause.

Result? Mental fog. Miscommunications. Mood swings. Mistaken texts. Memory gaps. Meltdowns in Target. These cosmic glitches hit differently based on which planet is in retrograde—and your personal birth chart.

The Retrograde Survival Strain Guide

◈ Mercury Retrograde (3-4x/year)

Rules: Communication, travel, technology, thoughts

Symptoms: Text fails, dropped Zoom calls, mental overload, overthinking

Cannabis Remedy:

- **Strain:** *Blue Dream* – Balanced, clear-headed, lightly euphoric
- **Why:** Calms mental static while keeping you conversational
- **Delivery:** Vape for clarity without couchlock
  Backup Strain: *Super Lemon Haze* – Mental alertness with a sunny edge

Pro Tip: Triple-check texts before sending. And don't respond to *"U up?"*

♀ Venus Retrograde (Every 18 months)

Rules: Love, beauty, money, relationships

Symptoms: Ex nostalgia, self-esteem dips, messy romance revisits

Cannabis Remedy:

- **Strain:** *Strawberry Cough* – Uplifting and confidence-boosting
- **Why:** Lightens heartache and restores your inner glow
- **Delivery:** Joint or rose-petal pre-roll for romantic ritual
  Backup Strain: *Wedding Cake* – Sweet, social, emotionally softening

Pro Tip: Don't text your ex. Roll a self-love blunt instead and put on your finest playlist.

♂ **Mars Retrograde (Every 2 years)**

Rules: Drive, ambition, anger, conflict

Symptoms: Low energy, passive-aggression, weird fights, irritability

Cannabis Remedy:

- **Strain:** *Northern Lights* – Calming, sedative, peaceful
- **Why:** Quiets frustration and restores internal momentum
- **Delivery:** Edible or nighttime tincture
  Backup Strain: *Purple Punch* – Sweet chill with just enough mood lift

Pro Tip: Channel that fire into stretching, art, or controlled video game rage. Not text arguments.

◈ Jupiter Retrograde (Annually)

Rules: Expansion, abundance, beliefs, big-picture goals

Symptoms: Loss of direction, doubt in path, philosophical spiraling

Cannabis Remedy:

- **Strain:** *Durban Poison* – Clear-headed and visionary
- **Why:** Enhances optimism while keeping ideas flowing
- **Delivery:** Sativa-rich flower or energetic gummy
  Backup Strain: *Pineapple Express* – Light, adventurous, joyful

Pro Tip: Use this time to journal about your *real* goals. Don't worry, the high will help.

◈ Saturn Retrograde (Annually)

Rules: Discipline, structure, responsibility, karma

Symptoms: Overwhelm, fear of failure, life audits

Cannabis Remedy:

- **Strain:** *Harlequin (CBD dominant)* – Functional and grounding
- **Why:** Calms pressure while enhancing clarity
- **Delivery:** CBD joint, or 1:1 tincture for daytime use
  Backup Strain: *ACDC* – Focused and anxiety-friendly

Pro Tip: Break big tasks into little ones. Light up when the inner critic talks too loud.

⬦ Uranus Retrograde (Annually)

Rules: Change, innovation, rebellion, chaos

Symptoms: Random disruptions, restlessness, tech burnout

Cannabis Remedy:

- **Strain:** *Jack Herer* – Bright and mentally stimulating
- **Why:** Tames rebellion into innovation
- **Delivery:** Daytime flower, perfect for creative rebellion
  Backup Strain: *Sour Diesel* – For breaking through mental blocks

Pro Tip: Set healthy digital boundaries. Then microdose genius.

◈ Neptune Retrograde (Annually)

Rules: Dreams, illusions, intuition, subconscious

Symptoms: Vivid dreams, delusions cracking, spiritual fog

Cannabis Remedy:

- **Strain:** *Skywalker OG* – Trippy, contemplative, slightly sleepy
- **Why:** Enhances the mystical without spiraling into disillusion
- **Delivery:** Bong or moonlight blunt
  Backup Strain: *Lavender Kush* – Dreamy, gentle, emotionally soothing

Pro Tip: Keep a dream journal near your nightstand. Or your snack drawer.

⬦ **Pluto Retrograde (Annually)**

Rules: Power, transformation, shadow work, trauma

Symptoms: Emotional dredging, control issues, ego breakdowns

Cannabis Remedy:

- **Strain:** *LSD (strain)* – Psychedelic edge without losing reality
- **Why:** Supports deep self-reflection with symbolic insights
- **Delivery:** Best in a sacred solo ritual setting
  Backup Strain: *Death Star* – Deep, dark, but not overpowering

Pro Tip: You're not broken—you're becoming. This is your cocoon. Light up and face the mirror.

Bonus: Creating a Retrograde Rescue Kit
Keep these on hand all retrograde season:

- High-CBD strain (Harlequin or ACDC)
- One sativa (Durban Poison or Lemon Haze)
- One indica (Northern Lights or Lavender Kush)
- Rolling papers + backup lighter
- Journal or voice memo app
- Cleansing tools: sage, palo santo, sound bowl
- Playlist: Retrograde Chill & Heal Mix

Final Puff: Don't Fear the Retrograde—Smoke Through It
The universe isn't out to get you—it's pushing pause so you can *reflect*. With the right cannabis companion, you can move through these planetary rewinds with grace, clarity, and even laughter. Think of your chosen strain as a celestial translator, helping you decode the lessons,

soothe the friction, and maybe even spark some creative breakthroughs along the way.

Next time Mercury messes up your texts, just smile, spark up, and say: "Not today, cosmos."

Chapter 17: The Four Elements High – Fire, Earth, Air, Water

Breathe, Burn, Flow, Root—The High is Elemental

In astrology and spirituality, the universe is composed of four fundamental energies: Fire, Earth, Air, and Water. These aren't just poetic ideas—they're archetypes of personality, mood, intention, and even *how* we get high.

The four elements influence how we engage with cannabis, from strain preference to smoking method, from music choice to snack style. Some signs want to get hyped and yell at the stars. Others want to melt into a mossy bean bag and vibe to rainforest sounds. One thing's for sure: *your element shapes your buzz.*

In this chapter, we'll explore the elemental personalities, their cannabis preferences, and how to design the perfect session for each. Whether you're a Fire Sign torching the blunt of destiny or a Water Sign soaking in an infused bath with seaweed edibles, this guide brings you back to nature—highly.

◈ **Fire Signs – Aries, Leo, Sagittarius**

Elemental Mood: Action. Inspiration. Confidence. Loud vibes and spontaneous highs.

Signature Traits: Passionate, daring, bold, sometimes impulsive, always the life of the session.

◈ **Fire's Cannabis Personality:**

- Craves fast-acting strains that elevate mood and spark motion.
- Loves group energy, dancing, laughing, and taking charge.
- May over-smoke if unchecked (they *really* like to win the blunt rotation).

◈ **Best Strains:**

- **Pineapple Express** – Energetic, cinematic, and uplifting.
- **Green Crack** – Instant alertness, ideal for creative outbursts.
- **Super Silver Haze** – Mental clarity with a firebrand kick.

◈ **Ritual Tips:**

- **Method:** Blunts or joints passed in circle—group energy required.
- **Setting:** Rooftop party, late-night bonfire, festival parking lot.
- **Snack Vibe:** Spicy chips, street tacos, or anything dramatic and messy.
- **Fire Sign Affirmation:** "I burn bright, and everyone around me feels the warmth."

◈ Earth Signs – Taurus, Virgo, Capricorn

Elemental Mood: Grounded. Stable. Sensory. Controlled highs and curated snacks.

Signature Traits: Practical, refined, and secretly sensual. Earth signs know exactly how high they *want* to be—and they'll stop there.

◈ Earth's Cannabis Personality:

- Enjoys functional, body-centered strains that enhance relaxation or productivity.
- Prefers consistency: the same strain, the same brand, the same routine.
- Can be the "herbalist" of the group—always educated on cannabinoids.

◈ Best Strains:

- **Northern Lights** – Deep body calm without sedation.
- **Blue Cheese** – Rich flavor, mental ease, and grounded chill.
- **Harlequin** – CBD-rich and emotionally balancing.

◈ Ritual Tips:

- **Method:** Edibles or pipe—precise, planned, and measured.
- **Setting:** A clean, candlelit room with cozy textures and earthy music.
- **Snack Vibe:** Charcuterie board, herbal tea, chocolate-dipped strawberries.
- **Earth Sign Affirmation:** "I ground my energy and bloom in peace."

◈ **Air Signs – Gemini, Libra, Aquarius**

Elemental Mood: Curious. Mental. Experimental. Highs full of tangents, laughter, and light speed thought.

Signature Traits: Talkative, witty, idea-driven, slightly chaotic. Air signs get high to think *more*—not less.

◈ **Air's Cannabis Personality:**

- Craves heady, cerebral highs that spark conversation and inspire weird ideas.
- Loves experimenting with new strains, tools, and smoke tricks.
- Might forget they're holding the joint while mid-story.

◈ **Best Strains:**

- **Jack Herer** – Creative, clear-headed, perfect for sharing weird theories.
- **Lemon Haze** – Citrus-bright focus with a giggly finish.
- **Chocolope** – Spiraling ideas and intellectual joy.

◈ **Ritual Tips:**

- **Method:** Vape pen or gravity bong—anything futuristic or gadget-like.
- **Setting:** Bookstore cafe, record shop, retro lounge, starlit balcony.
- **Snack Vibe:** Macarons, trail mix, or absurdly specific cereal brands.
- **Air Sign Affirmation:** "I rise with thought, speak with light, and drift with delight."

◈ **Water Signs – Cancer, Scorpio, Pisces**

Elemental Mood: Emotional. Intuitive. Dreamy. Cannabis as ritual, mood enhancer, or spiritual key.

Signature Traits: Deep feelers, nostalgia explorers, and romantic thinkers. Water signs use cannabis like incense—for memory, mood, and soulwork.

◈ **Water's Cannabis Personality:**

- Favors strains that facilitate introspection, mood enhancement, and sensory immersion.
- Loves to smoke alone or in small sacred circles.
- Tends to cry, laugh, or astral project mid-high (and all three are valid).

◈ **Best Strains:**

- **Lavender Kush** – Gentle, floral, soul-soothing.
- **Skywalker OG** – Floaty and emotionally meditative.
- **Blueberry** – Safe, nostalgic, and emotionally lush.

◈ **Ritual Tips:**

- **Method:** Bong hits during bath time or moonlight joints with crystals nearby.
- **Setting:** Garden at dusk, oceanfront cottage, or your bed surrounded by pillows.
- **Snack Vibe:** Sea salt chocolate, chamomile shortbread, watermelon slices.
- **Water Sign Affirmation:** "I flow where intuition leads. I feel. I heal. I float."

◈ Blending Elements in a Group Sesh

Each element adds essential flavor to a group smoke circle:

Element	Role in the Circle	Watch Out For
Fire	The energy spark	Hogging the joint
Earth	The stabilizer	Being too rigid with routine
Air	The idea generator	Forgetting snacks and losing lighters
Water	The vibe keeper	Crying during a cartoon and making it everyone's problem

Creating elemental balance means you'll have someone to light it, someone to plan it, someone to talk through it, and someone to feel it deeply.

◈ How to Discover Your Elemental Signature

- **Sun Sign:** Your core energy
- **Moon Sign:** Emotional cannabis response
- **Rising Sign:** Your high behavior in social settings

For example:

- A Capricorn Sun, Scorpio Moon, Gemini Rising = Earth-Water-Air
- This person gets high to relax (Earth), might cry during Planet Earth (Water), and loves talking about aliens (Air).

Understanding your elemental trinity can help you *curate your own strain blend* for mind, body, and spirit.

Final Puff: The Elements Don't Just Guide You—They *Get You High* Too

Fire inspires the spark. Earth contains it. Air fans it. Water cools it. Each element holds a vibration—and when cannabis enters the ritual, it becomes a sensory amplifier of that elemental force. Smoke like a flame. Chill like a stone. Think like the wind. Flow like a river.

No matter your sign, your element is your cosmic cannabis guide.

Chapter 18: Cannabis Rituals by the Moon Phases

The Moon, the Bud, and the Ritual

The Moon has always been the great orchestrator of rhythm—tides rise to greet her pull, seeds germinate by her light, and witches cast spells when she's at her brightest. But did you know your cannabis rituals can be aligned with her phases to deepen your high, magnify intention, and enhance emotional flow?

Pairing **moon magick with cannabis** isn't just poetic—it's *powerful*. Each moon phase carries distinct energy, and cannabis acts as a botanical amplifier. Whether you're setting goals, shedding emotional weight, or simply stargazing with a sacred joint, syncing with lunar phases turns every puff into a planetary prayer.

This chapter breaks down each moon phase—what it means, how it affects your vibe, and how to elevate your cannabis experience accordingly.

◈ **New Moon – Seed the Smoke**

Vibe: New beginnings, intention-setting, inner quiet

Energy: Yin, introspective, dark and fertile

Cannabis Ritual Theme: Dreaming + seeding

Best Strains:

- *Afghan Kush* – Grounding and restful
- *Lavender Kush* – Dreamy and gentle
- *CBD-heavy blends* – For clarity and calm vision-setting

Ritual Suggestions:

- Write down three goals while holding your chosen bud or joint
- Inhale while visualizing seeds sprouting with every puff
- Exhale self-doubt into the darkness

Mantra: *"In this stillness, I plant sacred beginnings."*

◈ **Waxing Crescent – Build the Buzz**

Vibe: Motivation, commitment, action planning

Energy: Gaining momentum, fresh energy flow

Cannabis Ritual Theme: Amplify + energize

Best Strains:

- *Super Lemon Haze* – Bright and focused
- *Durban Poison* – Mental clarity and joy
- *Jack Herer* – Visionary and motivating

Ritual Suggestions:

- Light a candle and toke while making a vision board
- Speak your goals aloud between hits
- Journal what action feels most aligned

Mantra: *"I grow stronger with every inhale of intention."*

◈ **First Quarter – Push Through Resistance**

Vibe: Overcoming blocks, bold decisions

Energy: Determined, courageous, friction-based

Cannabis Ritual Theme: Breakthrough + movement

Best Strains:

- *Green Crack* – High energy, productivity
- *Blue Dream* – Balances mental strength with emotional grace
- *Space Queen* – Quirky and clears roadblocks

Ritual Suggestions:

- Smoke before taking one action you've been avoiding
- Burn a written fear or doubt
- Combine cannabis with a power playlist and dance it out

Mantra: *"I blaze through obstacles with sacred fire."*

◈ Waxing Gibbous – Refine the Ritual

Vibe: Patience, reevaluation, detail work

Energy: Almost-there, strategic, contemplative

Cannabis Ritual Theme: Adjust + align

Best Strains:

- *Harlequin* – Balanced, focused, meditative
- *ACDC* – Mild and emotionally stabilizing
- *Northern Lights* – Smooth contemplation

Ritual Suggestions:

- Review your goals—what needs tweaking?
- Microdose while editing a project or making refinements
- Try a cannabis bath soak with essential oils and soft lighting

Mantra: *"I align my actions with divine timing."*

◈ Full Moon – Illuminate and Elevate

Vibe: Celebration, clarity, culmination

Energy: Hypercharge, completion, magic magnified

Cannabis Ritual Theme: Manifest + radiate

Best Strains:

- *Skywalker OG* – Cosmic expansion
- *Pineapple Express* – Euphoric celebration
- *Strawberry Cough* – Social and vibrant

Ritual Suggestions:

- Hold a full moon smoke circle with friends
- Charge your cannabis under moonlight in a glass jar
- Write a thank-you letter to yourself for how far you've come—then toke and read it aloud

Mantra: *"I inhale gratitude, I exhale radiance."*

◈ **Waning Gibbous – Release with Grace**

Vibe: Letting go, sharing wisdom, reflecting

Energy: Softening, processing, giving

Cannabis Ritual Theme: Reflect + release

Best Strains:

- *Lavender Kush* – Deep release and comfort
- *Granddaddy Purple* – Heavy emotional surrender
- *Blueberry* – Emotional sweetness, healing

Ritual Suggestions:

- Write down one thing you're ready to let go of—burn it
- Meditate with smoke rising and imagine your tension floating upward
- Have a slow solo session with a nostalgic playlist

Mantra: *"What no longer serves me gently fades into smoke."*

⬖ Last Quarter – Cleanse and Reclaim

Vibe: Release, clearing, turning inward

Energy: Purification, renewal

Cannabis Ritual Theme: Detox + reset

Best Strains:

- *CBD-dominant strains* – Clean, clear, light
- *Northern Lights* – Restful and purifying
- *Jack Herer (microdose)* – To keep clarity while cleansing

Ritual Suggestions:

- Clean your bong, reorganize your stash
- Detox from social media or negative environments
- Combine cannabis with a decluttering session or smoke with windows open

Mantra: *"I cleanse my space, body, and mind."*

◈ **Waning Crescent – Rest and Surrender**

Vibe: Deep rest, reflection, spiritual preparation

Energy: Surrender, spiritual closure, hibernation

Cannabis Ritual Theme: Rest + renew

Best Strains:

- *Purple Punch* – Sleepy and soul-deep
- *Skywalker OG* – Astral journey friendly
- *Lavender Kush* – For ultimate surrender

Ritual Suggestions:

- Prepare cannabis-infused herbal tea for night use
- Journal your dreams or visit your "inner sanctuary" through meditation
- Rest in silence with ambient music and a calming smoke

Mantra: *"I trust the darkness as the beginning of my next light."*

◈ The Lunar Loop – Monthly Ritual Map

Moon Phase	Focus	Best Strain	Ritual Type
New Moon	Begin	Afghan Kush	Journaling + Intention
Waxing Crescent	Build	Super Lemon Haze	Vision board
First Quarter	Act	Green Crack	Breakthrough dance
Waxing Gibbous	Refine	Harlequin	Bath + editing
Full Moon	Celebrate	Skywalker OG	Smoke circle + gratitude
Waning Gibbous	Reflect	Blueberry	Release ritual
Last Quarter	Cleanse	Northern Lights	Space clearing
Waning Crescent	Rest	Purple Punch	Sleep prep + surrender

Final Puff: Smoke with the Moon, Shift with the Universe

The Moon will keep rising and falling whether you notice her or not—but when you *do*, and you *align your cannabis rituals with her phases*, everything begins to move with sacred timing. You become more aware, more intentional, more in sync with nature's beat.

So roll with her rhythms, toke with the tides, and let the Moon be your guide through every high.

Chapter 19: Stoner Horoscopes for Each Sign

Welcome to the HighScope

Every zodiac sign has a unique energetic rhythm—and when cannabis enters the picture, that rhythm gets amplified, redirected, or hilariously derailed. These *Stoner Horoscopes* aren't your average astroforecast. They're personalized, smoke-infused glimpses into the vibe of your cosmic path, filtered through terpenes, munchies, and spiritual side quests.

Whether you're looking for your best smoking day, avoiding emotional landmines, or seeking the perfect strain match for your week, this is your **planetary weed weather report**. Let the stars guide your sessions and the herb elevate your horoscope.

◈ Aries – The Blazing Trailblazer

Forecast: This week, your fire needs focus. Slow your smoke roll—impulsivity might lead you to eat an entire box of cereal *and* start three unfinished projects. A heady sativa will get you amped, but try balancing it with breathwork.

Best Days to Smoke: Tuesday and Saturday

Avoid: Arguing while high—it'll feel justified, but probably isn't

Weekly Strain Match: *Super Silver Haze* – for fiery initiative without burnout

Stoner Tip: Start the project *after* the blunt, not during.

◈ Taurus – The Cozy Connoisseur

Forecast: Indulgence calls, and you're more than ready to answer. This is the perfect time for body highs, soft blankets, and gourmet snacks. Don't mistake isolation for solitude—invite someone into your chill zone. Or your blunt rotation.

Best Days to Smoke: Friday and Sunday

Avoid: Eating your entire edible supply in one night

Weekly Strain Match: *Blueberry Kush* – lush, sweet, and grounding

Stoner Tip: Upgrade your snack game with infused truffle popcorn.

◈ Gemini – The High-Flying Hummingbird

Forecast: Mental fireworks ahead! Your brain's firing faster than a group chat at 2 a.m., so channel the chaos into something fun: voice memos, sketching, or spontaneous stoned rants. Just... try to remember where you left your lighter.

Best Days to Smoke: Wednesday and Saturday

Avoid: Oversharing while high (even *you* will cringe later)

Weekly Strain Match: *Chocolope* – for cosmic conversations and creative spirals

Stoner Tip: Keep a "high thoughts" journal—you're onto something.

◈ Cancer – The Sentimental Smoker

Forecast: Emotions are rippling under the surface like a stoned sea turtle gliding through nostalgia. Use this time for self-care rituals. Cannabis will heighten your intuition, so pay attention to your gut—and maybe call your mom.

Best Days to Smoke: Monday and Friday

Avoid: Listening to sad music while high unless you're ready to cry into your snack bowl

Weekly Strain Match: *Lavender Kush* – gentle, soothing, emotionally safe

Stoner Tip: Create a moonlit blanket fort and just *feel*.

◇ **Leo – The Starry-Eyed Showstopper**

Forecast: You're magnetic this week, Leo. Prepare to hold court—whether it's karaoke night, game night, or storytelling by the campfire. Your high will be dramatic, performative, and totally unforgettable. Just don't forget to pass the joint.

Best Days to Smoke: Thursday and Sunday

Avoid: Dominating the conversation without letting others riff

Weekly Strain Match: *Pineapple Express* – bold, animated, bright

Stoner Tip: Film a stoned TikTok dance. It'll go viral. (Maybe.)

⬦ Virgo – The Elevated Analyst

Forecast: You're craving clarity—and cannabis can be your sacred assistant. Microdosing will work wonders. Use your buzz to plan, clean, optimize, or design something niche and brilliant. Your mind wants order, and the smoke brings flow.

Best Days to Smoke: Tuesday and Friday

Avoid: Getting stuck editing that email for 40 minutes

Weekly Strain Match: *Harlequin* – clean, focused, and mentally balanced

Stoner Tip: Organize your stash like a sacred archive.

◈ Libra – The Harmonious High Priest

Forecast: This week is about aesthetic highs and emotional equilibrium. Seek beautiful settings, calming music, and artistic strain pairings. Decision-making may feel impossible, but that's okay—just flip a coin and vibe with the outcome.

Best Days to Smoke: Wednesday and Saturday

Avoid: Overcommitting to 4 different sesh invites—choose peace

Weekly Strain Match: *Strawberry Cough* – breezy and beautifully uplifting

Stoner Tip: Curate a "smoke aesthetic" and take it way too seriously.

◈ Scorpio – The Alchemical Smoker

Forecast: Intensity is rising. Cannabis might deepen your introspection, unearth repressed memories, or inspire transformative ideas. Handle this week like a sacred ceremony: journal, shadow work, and soul-level stoned epiphanies are likely.

Best Days to Smoke: Monday and Thursday

Avoid: Watching true crime while high—it'll spiral

Weekly Strain Match: *LSD (strain)* – introspective and just trippy enough

Stoner Tip: Create a private ritual space for "solo smoke shadows."

◈ Sagittarius – The Cosmic Explorer

Forecast: Adventure calls, and your blunt is your compass. Whether you're booking a trip, chasing a sunrise, or expanding your mind with stoned philosophy, you'll feel a spiritual buzz. Just don't wander too far without a charger or snacks.

Best Days to Smoke: Thursday and Sunday

Avoid: Overbooking your week with impulsive "yes" energy

Weekly Strain Match: *Durban Poison* – bright and expansive

Stoner Tip: Try a strain, then read a book on parallel universes. Just trust me.

◈ Capricorn – The Strategic Stoner

Forecast: Structure is your friend, even while stoned. This week, use cannabis to unwind with purpose. Smoke sessions can be a reward system, a brainstorming lab, or even part of your personal development plan. Yes, you can get high and still run the empire.

Best Days to Smoke: Tuesday and Saturday

Avoid: Judging others for their *less productive* highs

Weekly Strain Match: *Northern Lights* – steady, efficient, low drama

Stoner Tip: Build a business idea during a late-night edible trip.

◈ Aquarius – The Galactic Puff Prodigy

Forecast: Ideas are flying through your head like comets through a nebula. This week brings visionary highs and outsider genius vibes. You may invent a device, sketch a utopia, or channel messages from alien weed spirits.

Best Days to Smoke: Wednesday and Sunday

Avoid: Smoking before attending meetings—your brain is on Mars

Weekly Strain Match: *Jack Herer* – inventive, smooth, revolutionary

Stoner Tip: Build something while high—even if it's just a bizarre playlist.

◈ Pisces – The Mystic Toker

Forecast: Your dreams may become movies, and your smoke sessions may turn into spiritual awakenings. Be mindful of escapism—use cannabis for sacred surrender, not emotional drowning. This is a week for guided meditation, long baths, and ethereal munchies.

Best Days to Smoke: Monday and Friday

Avoid: Watching fantasy films while high—you *will* believe you're the protagonist

Weekly Strain Match: *Skywalker OG* – dreamy, transportive, cosmic

Stoner Tip: Let the bathwater run, the music play, and your third eye bloom.

Final Puff: The Stars Don't Lie—They're Just High

Each sign has its own weed signature, its own smoke rhythm. Some get loud. Some go inward. Some build empires. Some dream entire galaxies.

This week—and every week—let the cosmos roll your joints, light your path, and guide your high.

Chapter 20: Munchie Madness – Recipes by Zodiac

Feed the Sign, Fuel the Vibe

When the munchies hit, it's never just hunger—it's a *cosmic craving*. Each zodiac sign has a distinct flavor profile, eating ritual, and comfort-food craving when stoned. Some signs go for gourmet, others grab whatever's closest. Some want to bake. Others just want cheese.

In this chapter, we dive fork-first into the stars to explore **zodiac-inspired recipes** that perfectly match each sign's post-smoke appetite. These dishes aren't just delicious—they're designed to fuel the soul, honor your elemental cravings, and keep the vibes high and flavorful.

Each recipe features:

- **Why it matches your sign**
- **Flavor profiles**
- **Quick how-to prep instructions**
- **Vibe pairing suggestions** (music, mood, strain)

◈ **Aries – Spicy Inferno Nachos**

Why it Fits: Aries needs heat, action, and immediate gratification. They want bold spice and crunch—no waiting.

Flavor Profile: Fiery, cheesy, tangy.

Quick Recipe:

- Layer tortilla chips, pepper jack cheese, jalapeños, and chili flakes.
- Bake for 10 mins at 400°F.
- Top with sriracha sour cream and crushed red pepper.

Pair with: Upbeat music, *Pineapple Express*, and competitive stoned board games.

Pro Tip: Add hot Cheetos for extra crunch and firepower.

◈ Taurus – Truffle Mac & Cheese Bites

Why it Fits: Taurus lives for comfort and elegance. They want richness in every bite—without needing to stand up too much.

Flavor Profile: Creamy, savory, decadent.

Quick Recipe:

- Mix cooked elbow pasta, cheddar, parmesan, truffle oil, and a splash of cream.
- Spoon into muffin tin, top with breadcrumbs, and bake at 375°F for 20 mins.

Pair with: Earthy strains like *Blueberry Kush*, fuzzy blankets, and jazz instrumentals.

Pro Tip: Serve with honey-drizzled cornbread for bonus indulgence.

◈ Gemini – Pick-Your-Flavor Popcorn Bar

Why it Fits: Gemini's taste buds can't sit still. They crave variety, customization, and chaotic snack tables.

Flavor Profile: Salty, sweet, spicy—why not all three?

Quick Recipe:

- Make a big batch of plain popcorn.
- Create flavor stations: ranch powder, cinnamon sugar, garlic parm, chili lime, caramel drizzle.
- Let your high brain roam wild.

Pair with: *Chocolope*, lo-fi beats, and stoned debates about nothing.

Pro Tip: Mix multiple flavors in one bowl to spark a flavor revolution.

◈ Cancer – Nostalgia PB&J Grilled Sandwich

Why it Fits: Cancer loves emotional eating and childhood comfort. The soft warmth of grilled peanut butter and jelly hits their soul directly.

Flavor Profile: Sweet, gooey, familiar.

Quick Recipe:

- Butter the outside of white bread. Fill with PB&J.
- Grill on a skillet until golden.
- Slice diagonally for full nostalgic power.

Pair with: *Lavender Kush*, emotional movie soundtracks, and soft lighting.

Pro Tip: Add banana slices for extra childhood magic.

◈ Leo – Loaded Royal Burger Sliders

Why it Fits: Leo needs a meal that's as extra as they are. Think gourmet sliders that photograph well.

Flavor Profile: Bold, saucy, luxurious.

Quick Recipe:

- Grill mini beef or plant-based patties.
- Top with sharp cheddar, caramelized onions, pickles, and special sauce.
- Stack on buttery brioche buns.

Pair with: *Pineapple Express*, dramatic playlists, and mirror selfies.

Pro Tip: Serve with gold cocktail sticks. Make it a performance.

◈ Virgo – DIY Bento Snack Box

Why it Fits: Virgo craves order, clean bites, and snack variety. A personalized bento box is stoner heaven.

Flavor Profile: Balanced, nourishing, crisp.

Quick Recipe:

- Section your box with: cucumber sticks, hummus, cheese cubes, dark chocolate, and herb crackers.
- Add a CBD gummy or infused trail mix corner.

Pair with: *Harlequin*, classical piano, and a freshly cleaned room.

Pro Tip: Label each section with mini sticky notes if you're *really* in the mood.

◈ Libra – Rainbow Fruit & Chocolate Skewers

Why it Fits: Libra loves beauty, color, and sensual harmony. These skewers are easy, elegant, and Instagrammable.

Flavor Profile: Sweet, juicy, luxurious.

Quick Recipe:

- Skewer strawberries, pineapple, kiwi, blueberries, and marshmallows.
- Drizzle with melted dark chocolate or white chocolate.
- Chill until slightly firm.

Pair with: *Strawberry Cough*, chillhop music, and ambient fairy lights.

Pro Tip: Serve on glass plates with rose petals (yes, seriously).

◈ Scorpio – Midnight Chili Brownies

Why it Fits: Scorpio wants intensity, mystery, and a little heat. These dark chocolate brownies come with a surprise kick.

Flavor Profile: Rich, spicy, indulgent.

Quick Recipe:

- Prepare a standard brownie mix.
- Add a dash of cayenne pepper and cinnamon.
- Bake, cool, and dust with cocoa powder.

Pair with: *LSD strain*, noir films, and candlelight.

Pro Tip: Cut into crescent shapes for occult vibes.

◈ Sagittarius – Campfire S'mores Quesadilla

Why it Fits: Sagittarius loves campfire stories and absurd snacks. This gooey, portable treat satisfies wanderlust and hunger.

Flavor Profile: Sweet, melted, outdoorsy.

Quick Recipe:

- Fill a tortilla with marshmallows, chocolate chips, and crushed graham crackers.
- Fold and toast on a skillet until golden and melted.

Pair with: *Durban Poison*, bonfire playlists, and a sleeping bag on the porch.

Pro Tip: Add peanut butter or Nutella for global expansion.

◈ **Capricorn – Elevated Herb & Cheese Crackers**

Why it Fits: Capricorns like functional, elevated bites. These are efficient, classy, and pair well with cannabis-fueled productivity.

Flavor Profile: Savory, herbed, crunchy.

Quick Recipe:

- Top artisan crackers with goat cheese, thyme, and honey drizzle.
- Optional: cannabis-infused honey or oil if desired.

Pair with: *Northern Lights*, ambient jazz, and goal-setting journals.

Pro Tip: Stack vertically and serve on a slate board for that CEO aesthetic.

◈ Aquarius – Galactic Trail Mix

Why it Fits: Aquarius needs something weird, spacey, and portable. This trail mix defies logic in the tastiest way.

Flavor Profile: Salty, sweet, eclectic.

Quick Recipe:

- Mix dried mango, spicy wasabi peas, pretzels, gummy bears, dark chocolate nibs, and granola clusters.
- Bonus: Add CBD-infused dried fruit or star-shaped candies.

Pair with: *Jack Herer*, space synth music, and a conspiracy podcast.

Pro Tip: Store it in a mason jar labeled "Fuel for Galactic Travel."

◈ Pisces – Dreamy Blue Milkshake Float

Why it Fits: Pisces craves something dreamy, liquid, and nostalgic. This blue-hued milkshake feels like an oceanic fantasy.

Flavor Profile: Creamy, sweet, magical.

Quick Recipe:

- Blend vanilla ice cream, milk, blue spirulina or food coloring, and a dash of vanilla extract.
- Top with whipped cream, edible glitter, and a gummy fish or two.

Pair with: *Skywalker OG*, ambient waves, and a bathtub full of pillows.

Pro Tip: Serve with a striped straw and call it a "Mermaid Potion."

Final Puff: You Are What You Eat (When You're High)

Food becomes sacred when paired with cannabis and aligned with your astrological cravings. Whether you're building your snack altar or prepping for the ultimate smoke feast, your sun sign can guide every delicious detail.

Smoke up. Chow down. Cosmic cravings approved.

Chapter 21: Cannabis & Compatibility

Love, Laughter, and the Sacred Puff

Romance under the stars is already electric—but introduce cannabis into the dynamic, and it becomes a cosmic firework show... or a hazy miscommunication spiral. Just like astrology reveals how sun signs interact emotionally and intellectually, it can also show how two people vibe together when they're high.

Some signs sync up like a perfect joint rotation—smooth, steady, euphoric. Others? Not so much. They drop lighters, clash on edible dosage, or argue over which strain to choose. This chapter explores **stoner relationship dynamics**, revealing which signs make for *passionate puff partners*, which might spark *fiery friction*, and how to navigate love through smoke.

Whether you're looking for your cannabis-compatible soulmate or trying to survive a blunt session with your opposite sign, this chapter has your high-hearted answers.

◈ **Fire Signs (Aries, Leo, Sagittarius)**

Passionate. Impulsive. Magnetic.

- **When Paired Together:** Prepare for bold adventures, spontaneous smoke sessions, and possibly a heated argument about who sparked the blunt. Their shared energy is intoxicating—until someone storms off mid-sesh.
- **Best Compatibility With:** Air signs (Gemini, Libra, Aquarius) who can fan the flames without getting burned.
- **Clash Warnings:** With Earth signs—who might find Fire signs exhausting—and with each other when egos collide.

Smoke Signal Soulmate: *Gemini for Aries, Libra for Leo, Aquarius for Sagittarius*

Relationship Ritual: Smoke under the stars after a hike, then plan your next big adventure—while very, very stoned.

◈ **Earth Signs (Taurus, Virgo, Capricorn)**

Grounded. Practical. Sensual.

- **When Paired Together:** Expect deeply sensual highs, carefully curated strain selections, and snack spreads worthy of royalty. Earth signs bond over slow-burning trust, but arguments may arise over routines or who's hogging the joint.
- **Best Compatibility With:** Water signs (Cancer, Scorpio, Pisces), who bring emotional depth and fluidity to Earth's structure.
- **Clash Warnings:** With Air signs, who may seem too unpredictable—or Fire signs who bring too much chaos.

Smoke Signal Soulmate: *Cancer for Taurus, Pisces for Virgo, Scorpio for Capricorn*

Relationship Ritual: Light up in a perfectly tidy space, followed by a stoned puzzle night and homemade infused snacks.

◈ **Air Signs (Gemini, Libra, Aquarius)**

Curious. Verbal. Inventive.

- **When Paired Together:** Conversations will be non-stop. Expect philosophical stoner chats, spontaneous poetry, playlist sharing, and joint-rolling competitions. Their high compatibility comes from shared mental stimulation and experimental smoke rituals.
- **Best Compatibility With:** Fire signs, who ignite their minds and push them to act on their many ideas.
- **Clash Warnings:** With Earth signs—Air signs crave change, and Earth signs resist it.

Smoke Signal Soulmate: *Sagittarius for Gemini, Leo for Libra, Aries for Aquarius*

Relationship Ritual: Joint journaling, passing a blunt during tarot readings, or inventing a new smoke game together.

◇ **Water Signs (Cancer, Scorpio, Pisces)**

Emotional. Intuitive. Transformative.

- **When Paired Together:** Deep. Emotional. Almost telepathic. Cannabis takes Water signs deeper into feeling, reflection, and vulnerability. They may share dreams, silent cuddles, or cry together mid-joint—and feel better afterward.
- **Best Compatibility With:** Earth signs for grounding and safety. They balance Water's tides with strong roots.
- **Clash Warnings:** With Fire signs, who may scorch their sensitivities—or Air signs who intellectualize what Water feels.

Smoke Signal Soulmate: *Taurus for Cancer, Capricorn for Scorpio, Virgo for Pisces*

Relationship Ritual: Infused bath rituals, dream journaling while high, or moonlit meditations together.

Pairing Highlights: Who Clicks and Who Crashes

Pairing	Cosmic High	Possible Crash
Aries + Gemini	Flirty, fun, adventurous	Impulsive energy overload
Taurus + Cancer	Deep comfort, perfect cuddle sessions	Emotional codependency
Leo + Libra	Glamorous, laughter-filled highs	Passive-aggressive power plays
Virgo + Capricorn	Productive, stoned building sessions	Too serious, too sober
Scorpio + Pisces	Spiritually sensual, deeply bonded	Emotional drowning if not grounded
Sagittarius + Aquarius	Philosophical and inventive	Detached chaos and overthinking

Clash Warnings – Smoke Caution Ahead

- **Aries + Scorpio:** Two alphas, one lighter—expect power struggles and jealousy in smoke form.
- **Leo + Virgo:** One craves attention, the other craves precision. Passive judgment ensues.
- **Gemini + Capricorn:** One talks through the high; the other's already building an LLC in their head.
- **Cancer + Aquarius:** One wants emotional connection, the other wants space. Conflict arises when empathy and aloofness meet.

Soulmate Sessions – When the Match is Divine

When cannabis flows between the *right* signs, it opens portals of connection. Conversations deepen. Silence becomes shared sacred space. Touch becomes electric. These pairings feel like two parts of the same blunt—designed to burn together:

- **Taurus + Pisces** – Earth holds Water while Water soothes Earth. Add cannabis, and it's sensual serenity.
- **Libra + Leo** – Balanced glam meets radiant love. Cannabis makes them feel like stoned royalty.
- **Sagittarius + Gemini** – Adventurous, hilarious, ever-changing. Their sessions are never boring—and usually involve spontaneous road trips.

Cannabis Love Language by Sign

Sign	Stoner Love Language
Aries	Bold initiation – they light it first and kiss you second
Taurus	Touch + Taste – back rubs and homemade munchies
Gemini	Words – endless high-convo cuddles
Cancer	Emotional presence – deep listening while passing the joint
Leo	Quality time – showing off + laughing together
Virgo	Acts of service – pre-rolls your joints and organizes the sesh
Libra	Aesthetic vibe – curates the candles and playlist
Scorpio	Intensity – deep eye contact between puffs
Sagittarius	Adventure – hotboxing a mountaintop
Capricorn	Reliability – shows up with snacks and rolling gear
Aquarius	Surprise – creates a new ritual every time

Sign	Stoner Love Language
Pisces	Dreaminess – lets you drift off on their chest mid-high

Final Puff: Love is a Shared High

Compatibility isn't about being the same—it's about complementing each other's frequencies. With cannabis in the mix, those frequencies amplify, revealing what's under the surface: affection, friction, empathy, misalignment, or deep soul resonance.

Whether you're looking for your smoke soulmate or decoding your partner's stoner quirks, remember: **love—like weed—hits better when it's shared, respected, and lit with intention.**

Chapter 22: Zodiac Edibles – Creative Infusions Inspired by the Stars

Star-Guided Munchies for the Elevated Soul

Edibles are more than just a cannabis delivery method—they're a ritual, a sensory experience, and (when aligned with your sign) a full-blown astrological ceremony. Every zodiac sign has a different approach to food and cannabis: some bake with precision, others toss ingredients together in a cosmic kitchen frenzy. Some signs seek bold flavors, while others long for comfort or nostalgia.

This chapter explores **DIY infused treats for each zodiac sign**, designed to match the personality, flavor palette, and planetary energy of the stars. From infused lavender cookies to fiery truffle popcorn, these edibles aren't just snacks—they're personalized *sacred bites*.

Each recipe includes:

- **Why it fits your sign**
- **Flavor profile**
- **Infusion method suggestion**
- **Best time to enjoy**

◈ Aries – Firecracker Cheese Bites

Why It Fits: Aries wants fast, spicy, and bold. No-nonsense and no wait time.

Flavor Profile: Hot, salty, and addictive.

Recipe:

- Cube pepper jack cheese
- Drizzle with cannabis-infused hot sauce or chili oil
- Chill, then stab with toothpicks like fire-kissed appetizers

Infusion Method: Use a THC tincture in homemade chili oil

Best Time to Eat: Right before launching into an impulsive adventure or gaming session.

◈ Taurus – Infused Dark Chocolate Truffles with Sea Salt

Why It Fits: Taurus craves luxury, indulgence, and sensual satisfaction.

Flavor Profile: Rich, creamy, salty-sweet.

Recipe:

- Melt dark chocolate with cannabis butter
- Stir in cream, chill, and roll into truffles
- Dust with sea salt, cocoa, or crushed pistachios

Infusion Method: Use high-quality cannabutter

Best Time to Eat: After a long bath, in bed, under three blankets.

◈ Gemini – Infused Gummy Mosaic

Why It Fits: Gemini needs options—something colorful, tactile, and fun.

Flavor Profile: Fruity, chewy, vibrant.

Recipe:

- Mix fruit juice, gelatin, and THC tincture
- Pour into assorted silicone molds: stars, moons, letters
- Set, then create mix-and-match flavor combos

Infusion Method: Tincture or infused syrup

Best Time to Eat: Before socializing or brainstorming a wild idea.

◇ Cancer – Baked Banana Bread Moon Muffins

Why It Fits: Cancer's edible needs comfort and homey vibes.

Flavor Profile: Sweet, moist, and warmly spiced.

Recipe:

- Mash ripe bananas, mix with flour, sugar, nutmeg, and cannabutter
- Pour into muffin tins
- Bake until golden and aromatic

Infusion Method: Use cannabutter and a hint of vanilla THC extract

Best Time to Eat: During a full moon night in pajamas with a pet.

◈ Leo – Infused Glitter Star Cookies

Why It Fits: Leo wants glam and grandeur, even in a cookie.

Flavor Profile: Vanilla, almond, with a dash of edible sparkle.

Recipe:

- Roll out sugar cookie dough with infused butter
- Cut into stars, lions, or crowns
- Frost with royal icing and edible glitter

Infusion Method: Cannabutter in the dough

Best Time to Eat: At your own party, with music blasting and selfies incoming.

◈ Virgo – Herb-Infused Trail Mix Bars

Why It Fits: Virgo craves functionality and focus.

Flavor Profile: Nutty, balanced, energizing.

Recipe:

- Mix oats, almond butter, flaxseeds, and dried fruit
- Blend with cannabis-infused coconut oil
- Press into bars and chill

Infusion Method: Infused coconut oil

Best Time to Eat: Midday, paired with tea and productivity.

◈ Libra – Strawberry Rose Cheesecake Bites

Why It Fits: Libra values harmony, beauty, and sweetness with sophistication.

Flavor Profile: Floral, fruity, creamy.

Recipe:

- Blend cream cheese, sugar, vanilla, and infused butter
- Layer onto graham cracker crust in mini molds
- Top with sliced strawberries and rose petal garnish

Infusion Method: Cannabutter or infused cream

Best Time to Eat: Sunset, candles lit, romantic playlist on loop.

◈ **Scorpio – Dark Cherry Blood Orange Sorbet**

Why It Fits: Scorpio seeks depth and sensual mystery.

Flavor Profile: Tart, dark, luxurious.

Recipe:

- Blend blood orange juice, dark cherries, sugar, and cannabis tincture
- Freeze until soft-serve texture emerges
- Serve in black glassware for full occult drama

Infusion Method: Tincture stirred into juice before freezing

Best Time to Eat: Late night during moon rituals or tarot sessions.

◈ Sagittarius – Infused Spiced Churro Bites

Why It Fits: Sagittarius loves bold spices and wild experiences.

Flavor Profile: Cinnamon sugar, crispy warmth, adventurous.

Recipe:

- Fry bite-sized dough pieces
- Toss in cinnamon sugar
- Drizzle with cannabis-infused caramel

Infusion Method: Infused caramel sauce

Best Time to Eat: Road trip break or right before a philosophical smoke circle.

◈ Capricorn – Espresso Brownie Power Squares

Why It Fits: Capricorn needs efficient indulgence that doubles as fuel.

Flavor Profile: Bittersweet chocolate, coffee kick.

Recipe:

- Bake brownie batter with espresso powder and cannabutter
- Cut into squares
- Optional: top with dark chocolate drizzle or gold leaf

Infusion Method: Cannabutter

Best Time to Eat: After crushing your to-do list or during work-from-home zen time.

◈ Aquarius – Lavender Lemon Cosmic Bars

Why It Fits: Aquarius seeks the unusual and ethereal.

Flavor Profile: Bright, floral, otherworldly.

Recipe:

- Make shortbread base with infused coconut oil
- Pour lemon-lavender custard on top
- Chill and dust with powdered sugar and stardust sprinkles

Infusion Method: Cannabis-infused coconut oil

Best Time to Eat: Stargazing with binaural beats and alien documentaries.

◈ Pisces – Infused Vanilla Cloud Pudding

Why It Fits: Pisces wants soft, dreamy, and emotionally healing edibles.

Flavor Profile: Light, creamy, calming.

Recipe:

- Blend vanilla pudding base with infused milk or cream
- Top with whipped cream, blue sugar, and edible stars
- Chill and serve in seashell dishes (if you're feeling extra)

Infusion Method: THC-infused milk or creamer

Best Time to Eat: While journaling, sketching, or drifting into dreams.

Final Puff: Baked by the Stars

Edibles become an act of sacred creation when tailored to your cosmic blueprint. Whether you're baking with purpose, playing with flavors, or just vibing out in the kitchen, aligning your high with your sign's edible energy takes munchie moments to divine heights.

Create, infuse, and bite into your birthright. The stars are hungry—and so are you.

Chapter 23: The Astrology of Growing Cannabis

Growing with the Stars: Why Astrology Matters in Cultivation

Cannabis is more than a plant—it's a cosmic entity, deeply responsive to the rhythms of nature, light, and lunar cycles. Since ancient times, farmers have relied on the sky to time their crops. When it comes to cannabis, aligning your grow with astrological wisdom not only deepens your spiritual connection to the plant but can also result in stronger yields, more potent buds, and a more harmonious cultivation experience.

This chapter explores **which astrological signs, moon phases, and planetary influences** are most beneficial for cannabis cultivation—from seed to harvest. Whether you're a small-batch home grower or an herbal alchemist with spiritual leanings, this chapter will help you understand the **celestial science behind growing cannabis intentionally**.

◈ The Moon Phases and Cannabis Cultivation

The Moon governs water, root development, and feminine energy—all crucial in growing. Here's how each phase influences cannabis:

◈ New Moon – Intention & Planning

- Best for: Setting grow goals, cleansing the grow space, preparing soil.
- Energy: Quiet, reflective, dormant. Seeds planted now may have slow starts but carry potent energy.

◈ Waxing Crescent to First Quarter – Germination & Early Growth

- Best for: Planting seeds, rooting clones, stimulating leaf development.
- Energy: Expansion, vitality, increasing life force.

◈ Waxing Gibbous to Full Moon – Flowering & Nutrient Absorption

- Best for: Transplanting, watering, feeding, trellising.
- Energy: Peak moisture levels, strong cell growth, energy rises into the flowers.

◈ Full Moon – Bud & Bloom Boost

- Best for: Boosting terpene and cannabinoid development. Powerful time for flowering stage.
- Energy: High potency, spiritual alignment, increased energy flow.

◈ Waning Gibbous to Last Quarter – Pruning & Pest Control

- Best for: Removing dead leaves, organic pest treatments, gentle trimming.
- Energy: Drawing energy downwards into the roots. Detox phase.

◈ Waning Crescent – Harvesting & Drying

- Best for: Harvesting for flavor, potency, and preservation.
- Energy: Grounded, stable, perfect for final steps in the growing cycle.

◈ Best Zodiac Signs for Growing Activities

Each zodiac sign governs a part of the plant and offers unique growing benefits. These signs are used in **biodynamic agriculture**, and cannabis is no exception.

Zodiac Sign	Element	Governs	Best For
Taurus	Earth	Roots, stability	Ideal for planting and transplanting
Cancer	Water	Leaf growth, moisture	Great for germination and watering
Virgo	Earth	Organization, detail	Perfect for pruning, pest control
Scorpio	Water	Deep roots, potency	Enhances resin and trichome production
Sagittarius	Fire	Expansion, vitality	Boosts height and stretching phase
Capricorn	Earth	Structure, hardiness	Excellent for supporting stalks and resilience

Zodiac Sign	Element	Governs	Best For
Pisces	Water	Spirituality, final stages	Great for intuitive harvesting, moon rituals

Avoid:

- **Gemini, Aquarius, Leo** for germination or transplanting (these signs tend to bring airy or fiery instability).
- **Aries** for watering—too aggressive, may dry out plants.

◈ Planetary Influence on Cannabis Cultivation

- **Moon:** Controls growth speed, water intake, and flowering rhythm.
- **Venus:** Oversees taste, fragrance, sensuality—great for terpene development.
- **Mercury:** Boosts communication between roots and soil—ideal for nutrient absorption.
- **Saturn:** Governs discipline and time—good for drying, curing, and long-term storage planning.
- **Jupiter:** Expansive energy—plant during Jupiter transits for big yields.
- **Mars:** Governs energy and defense—great for pest-proofing and increasing strength.
- **Neptune:** Dreamy, best used for ceremonial growing, not practical tasks.

◈ **Cosmic Grow Calendar Overview**
Here's a sample grow calendar using lunar and zodiac timing:

January–February (Planning Phase):

- Cleanse grow space during waning moon in **Virgo**
- Set intentions during New Moon in **Capricorn**

March–April (Planting & Germination):

- Start seeds under **Waxing Moon in Cancer** or **Taurus**
- Avoid **Aries** moon for watering

May–June (Early Growth):

- Feed during Full Moon in **Scorpio**
- Prune with **Virgo** or **Capricorn** moon

July–August (Flowering):

- Boost flowering under Full Moon in **Sagittarius**
- Use **Pisces** moon for intuitive rituals

September–October (Harvest):

- Harvest during **Waning Moon in Pisces** or **Taurus**
- Begin curing process during **Last Quarter Moon in Virgo**

November–December (Reflection & Reset):

- Clean jars, tools, and plan next cycle
- Record notes under New Moon in **Sagittarius** or **Aquarius**

◈ Ritual Tips for Star-Aligned Growers

- **Moon Water Spray:** Charge water under a full moon in Cancer or Pisces and mist your plants gently.
- **Infused Grow Crystals:** Place green aventurine or moss agate in your soil for energy amplification.
- **Grow Journaling:** Note astrology during major plant events—harvests under certain moons may repeat patterns.
- **Grow Altar:** Build a small altar near your grow with elements aligned to your sign, moon phase, and intention (e.g., soil for Earth signs, candles for Fire).

◈ Final Puff: Plant What the Stars Whisper

When you grow cannabis in sync with the stars, you enter an ancient rhythm of earth and cosmos. Your plants are not just crops—they become spiritual allies, herbal companions, and symbols of your connection to the celestial cycles that birthed you.

Cultivate not just *weed*, but *wisdom*.

Chapter 24: The 13th Sign Controversy – Ophiuchus Highs & Hiccups

◈ Enter Ophiuchus: The High Nobody Invited (But Still Showed Up)

Ophiuchus—the mysterious serpent bearer—slinks into the room like that friend who wasn't technically invited to your smoke sesh, but shows up anyway with weird edibles and a lot of opinions. For decades, astrologers and astronomers have debated whether Ophiuchus deserves a place in the zodiac line-up. Some say it's the true 13th sign, nestled between Scorpio and Sagittarius. Others claim it's an interloper, a celestial squatter who just wants to crash on the zodiac's couch.

But in the world of **Cosmic Cannabis**, we believe in giving everyone a puff. So light one up and let's explore the high—and the hiccups—of being an Ophiuchus.

◈ So... Who *Is* Ophiuchus?

- **Dates:** November 29 – December 17 (according to some systems)
- **Symbol:** The Serpent Bearer (yes, really)
- **Element (Unofficially):** Fire meets Water with a twist of cosmic chaos
- **Vibe:** Mysterious, philosophical, a bit intense, healer with a god complex
- **Ruled By:** Asclepius, the Greek god of medicine—basically the zodiac's cannabis alchemist

Ophiuchus is associated with **spiritual rebirth, mysticism,** and **inner transformation.** They're like that one friend who microdoses psilocybin for "personal enlightenment" but won't stop monologuing about the root chakra during a group hotbox.

◈ Ophiuchus Highs – The Elevated Side of the Snake Bearer

- **Healer Energy:** They're the ones bringing essential oils and healing crystals to your sesh. And somehow, it works.
- **Mystical Intuition:** They can roll a joint by candlelight while interpreting tarot cards.
- **Cannabis Knowledge:** Knows the difference between limonene and pinene. Probably invented a strain named "Astral Rebirth OG."
- **Chill Alpha:** They command the room without raising their voice. You'll hand them the blunt even if you're not sure why.

Their Ideal Strain: *Snake's Kiss* – a fictional hybrid strain combining cerebral elevation with root chakra grounding. Earthy, citrusy, and with a slow-burning surprise ending.

◈◈ Ophiuchus Hiccups – The Cosmic Red Flags

- **Always Debating:** They'll interrupt your perfectly stoned monologue to "correct" the mythology of your sign.
- **Vibe Disruptor:** They might insist on burning sage *mid-session* or rearranging the furniture for "chi flow."
- **Edible Experiments:** Expect weed-infused kombucha or CBD-spiked mushroom broth. Results may vary.
- **Zodiac Interference:** Has probably tried to convince a Scorpio and a Sagittarius to "merge signs" and form a three-way relationship.

Warning: They might "accidentally" realign your chakras while you're just trying to eat Flaming Hot Cheetos and vibe.

◈ What Happens to the Other Signs If Ophiuchus Joins the Club?

Let's get real: adding a 13th sign is like trying to introduce a new stoner into a tight-knit smoke circle. It changes the rhythm, the rotation, and the energy. Here's how the rest of the zodiac feels about Ophiuchus crashing the sesh:

Sign	Reaction
Aries	"Who even invited this guy?"
Taurus	"If he touches my snacks, I swear—"
Gemini	"Finally, someone new to talk to!"
Cancer	*Cries softly in the corner because everything's changing*
Leo	"This is *my* spotlight. Get your own serpent."
Virgo	"There are twelve signs for a reason. Read the manual."
Libra	"So... do we get a new crystal color or what?"
Scorpio	"He's standing on my turf. I see you, snake boy."
Sagittarius	"He stole my birthday window. I demand a rematch."
Capricorn	"This complicates the calendar. I'm filing a complaint."

Sign	Reaction
Aquarius	"New sign? Fascinating. Let's make a podcast."
Pisces	"Ophiuchus? I dreamed about him last week."

◈ Ophiuchus vs. Scorpio & Sagittarius: The Cosmic Tug-of-Rotation

Scorpio and Sagittarius are the signs most impacted by Ophiuchus's alleged rise to zodiac power.

- **Scorpio feels dethroned:** "You can't just add a new brooding, mystical energy without consulting the council."
- **Sagittarius feels slighted:** "So he gets the bow and the snake? What's next, psychic archery?"

But Ophiuchus doesn't care. He's probably meditating in a hemp robe somewhere in the Andes while distilling terpenes from a cactus.

◈ Ophiuchus Rituals – If You Want to Channel the Serpent High

Want to embody Ophiuchus in your next cosmic session? Try this:

- **Strain Pairing:** Anything with "serpent," "soul," or "mystic" in the name. Look for hybrids with a cerebral twist.
- **Ritual Tools:** Snake incense holder, sacred herbs, a geode grinder, and a mirror for shadow reflection.
- **Ideal Setting:** A candlelit room with a tapestry of constellations and a snake-shaped joint holder.
- **Intention:** Self-reinvention. Smoke not just to relax—but to rewire your inner universe.

◈ **Cosmic Cannabis Theater Presents: "When Ophiuchus Entered the Zodiac Group Chat"**

Sagittarius: "Who is this guy?"

Ophiuchus: "I'm the 13th sign. The healer. The awakened one."

Scorpio: "He's standing where I stand."

Libra: "This is throwing off my aesthetic symmetry."

Gemini: "Hi! What's your moon sign? Do you like riddles?"

Aries: "If he takes my spark lighter, I'll fight him."

Pisces: "He's beautiful. I want to become him."

Ophiuchus: *"I am you."*

Cue dramatic puff of sage and slow exhale of cannabis mist.

◈ **Final Puff: Do You Need Ophiuchus in Your Chart?**

Not really. But should you invite him to your next smoke circle?

Absolutely.

Just make sure you hide the weird tea, label your edibles, and prepare for deep cosmic conversations about serpents, souls, and the metaphysical properties of rolling papers.

Chapter 25: The Cosmic Cannabis Code

◈ Inhale the Universe, Exhale Yourself

Across galaxies, herbs have always been vessels for wisdom, healing, and awakening. And cannabis? Cannabis is stardust you can smoke. It whispers in chlorophyll and breathes in spirals, just like your natal chart. The leaves curve like crescent moons, the pistils shimmer like sunflares, and every puff holds a lesson—custom-written by the cosmos.

You didn't stumble into your favorite strain by accident. You didn't choose your favorite toking ritual on a whim. Whether you lean toward earthy indicas under a Capricorn moon or prefer spontaneous sativa hits while Mercury dances through Gemini, your cannabis journey is astrologically coded.

Welcome to the final truth: **Your high is not random. It is your cosmic signature.**

◈ The 12 Keys of the Cosmic Cannabis Code

Let's distill the journey down to 12 universal truths—each shaped by a zodiac archetype but meant for *everyone*.

◈ Aries – The High Sparks Action

Your first puff is a match strike. You get ideas. You plan conquests. Cannabis awakens your *drive*—use it to start, not stall.

◈ Taurus – The High Grounds the Body

You are here. You are safe. Your snacks are sacred, your blanket a temple. Cannabis reconnects you to the body—honor it.

◈ Gemini – The High Unlocks Thought

Your mind dances. You speak in colors. Cannabis unzips the tongue and tickles synapses—use it to explore and share.

◈ Cancer – The High Heals the Heart

The bowl becomes a womb. You remember who you were. Cannabis softens grief and opens the chest—cry if needed.

◈ Leo – The High Amplifies the Self

You are art. You are voice. You are crown. Cannabis awakens the performer and the child—express, radiate, rejoice.

◈ Virgo – The High Orders Chaos

You clean. You sort. You realign. Cannabis, paradoxically, brings focus. Use it to structure your thoughts and rituals.

◈ Libra – The High Balances the Soul

Every toke is a scale balancing pleasure and peace. Cannabis is your harmonizer—use it for self-regulation and beauty-making.

◈ Scorpio – The High Reveals the Depths

Your demons arrive bearing gifts. You smoke and descend. Cannabis isn't always gentle—but it's always honest.

◈ Sagittarius – The High Expands the Horizon

You blaze and roam. You philosophize. Cannabis feeds your fire to know more—use it to chart new inner maps.

◈ Capricorn – The High Clarifies the Climb

You get strategic. Efficient. Visionary. Cannabis sharpens the blueprint—use it to merge purpose with peace.

◈ Aquarius – The High Sparks Innovation

You see patterns in the stars. You make playlists that sound like galaxies. Cannabis is your alien frequency—tune in.

◈ Pisces – The High Dissolves the Veil

You melt. You dream. You become everything and nothing. Cannabis is your mirror, muse, and mist—surrender.

◈ The Three Layers of Astrological High

1. **Sun Sign High:** Your core essence. This is how cannabis shapes your identity.
2. **Moon Sign High:** Your emotional trip. This is how you *feel* when you're elevated.
3. **Rising Sign High:** Your toking aesthetic. This is how you show up in a smoke circle.

Understanding all three opens the full code of how your soul dances with weed.

◈ Astro-Toke Philosophy: Smoke With Purpose

Here's a sacred truth most people miss: **Cannabis responds to consciousness.** Your intention before lighting up matters. So does the day, the moon phase, the planetary retrogrades, and even the sign your Venus is in.

Cannabis magnifies who you are *in that moment*. When you toke with purpose, you invite the stars to join the ritual.

Try this:

- Light up during your *solar return* (your birthday) and set a yearly vision.
- Toke during eclipses with a notebook in hand—record the wild truths that arrive.
- Use cannabis on your Saturn return to reflect and realign your karmic contract.
- Smoke at dawn during a Leo moon if you need courage. At dusk in Scorpio for healing.

◈ The Cannabis-DNA Link to the Cosmos

Let's take it further: THC molecules, like you, are carbon-based. Their structure mimics patterns found in nebulae and plant geometry. Some believe cannabis is an echo of a higher vibrational frequency—left on Earth as a tool, a transmitter, or a key.

The same way birth charts carry planetary coordinates of your soul, each cannabis strain carries its own energetic imprint. Indica strains ground. Sativas awaken. Hybrids harmonize. When you choose a strain intuitively, you're performing *cosmic alchemy*—blending the stars outside you with the plant inside you.

◈ The Final Message

You are a celestial being in a human body holding a rolled prayer made of Earth and sky.

You are not *getting high*.

You are **activating alignment**.

You are remembering who you were before the world named you.

And you are doing it with the most sacred herbal ally available—one kissed by Venus, watched over by the Moon, and rooted in the ground of this rotating miracle we call home.

◈ Final Puff: You Were Born For This

Every sign. Every moon phase. Every bowl packed with loving intention.

You were born for this journey.

You are stardust, inhaled.

And your cannabis ritual is your celestial return ticket.

Go smoke your birthright.

Appendix A: Cannabis Strain Glossary

A curated guide to the most referenced strains in the book

Welcome to your celestial cannabis companion—a tailored glossary of the most referenced strains across *Cosmic Cannabis*. Each strain is more than a name; it's a mood, a message, and a molecular mirror reflecting your star-born personality. Use this guide to align your highs with your horoscope.

Each entry includes:

- **Primary Effects**
- **Flavor & Aroma Notes**
- **Astrological Sign Synergy**
- **Ideal Use Time / Ritual Setting**

◈ **Sour Diesel**

Primary Effects: Energetic, uplifting, cerebral clarity

Flavor Notes: Diesel, citrus zest, herbal brightness

Sign Synergy: Air signs (Gemini, Libra, Aquarius) thrive on this strain's speed-of-thought stimulation. It's the unofficial brainstorming booster of the zodiac.

Best Used For: Morning productivity rituals, moon journaling during Mercury direct, creative planning, or solving life's mysteries with a friend at 2AM.

◈ Granddaddy Purple (GDP)

Primary Effects: Deeply relaxing, body-numbing, euphoric sedation

Flavor Notes: Grape, berry, earth, floral musk

Sign Synergy: Earth signs (Taurus, Virgo, Capricorn) appreciate the grounded, luxurious stillness GDP brings. A favorite for post-achievement grounding or Taurus-style indulgence.

Best Used For: Rest days, emotional grounding after a long week, full moon body care, or watching slow documentaries while wrapped in velvet.

◈ **Blue Dream**

Primary Effects: Euphoric, balanced, uplifting yet chill

Flavor Notes: Sweet berry, vanilla, light herbal citrus

Sign Synergy: Universally adaptable—Blue Dream is the zodiac peacekeeper. Works well with most signs but especially bridges extremes like Pisces/Aries and Virgo/Libra.

Best Used For: Group smoke circles, creative flow states, dream journaling, casual spiritual rituals, or hybrid-mood evenings.

◈ **Green Crack**

Primary Effects: Laser-sharp focus, high energy, motivational uplift

Flavor Notes: Tropical fruit, mango, spice

Sign Synergy: Capricorn uses it to plan empires. **Sagittarius** lights up their wanderlust. Best for signs that need a boost to start or sustain big ideas.

Best Used For: Morning rituals, entrepreneurial brainstorming, physical organization, or finishing that passion project you started last retrograde.

◈ **Northern Lights**

Primary Effects: Sleepy, dreamy, introspective, full-body calm

Flavor Notes: Earthy pine, sweetness, mint

Sign Synergy: Pisces and **Cancer** feel cradled in cosmic arms with Northern Lights. A perfect nightcap for the emotionally or spiritually overwhelmed.

Best Used For: Deep meditation, moonlit solo sessions, intuitive journaling, or emotional reset after a heavy day.

◈ Harlequin

Primary Effects: Clear-headed, calm without sedation, high-CBD relief

Flavor Notes: Earth, mango, sweet musk

Sign Synergy: Virgo's best friend. Precise and non-intrusive, Harlequin is perfect for anxiety-prone signs or those needing clarity without fog. Also appreciated by Libra and Capricorn for balance.

Best Used For: Mid-day focus, tension relief, herbal self-care, or spiritual clarity rituals. Excellent for beginner star-born tokers.

◇ **Purple Haze**

Primary Effects: Energetic creativity, mild euphoria, trippy insight

Flavor Notes: Grape candy, spice, floral undertones

Sign Synergy: Aquarius adores the radical frequency shift. **Scorpio** uses it to open portals into poetic shadows. A perfect "third-eye opener."

Best Used For: Experimental art, stargazing, writing sci-fi under candlelight, or making an altar for forgotten gods.

◈ Durban Poison

Primary Effects: Social, alert, mentally activating

Flavor Notes: Sweet licorice, pine, citrus

Sign Synergy: Gemini and **Sagittarius** connect with its quick wit and open-hearted boldness. It's the "party philosopher" of the strain world.

Best Used For: High-vibe conversation, podcasting, group rituals, vision boarding with friends, or just talking to your houseplants (and getting answers).

◈ Final Puff – Using This Glossary in Real Life

- **Pair by Purpose:** Choose based on what the stars (and your soul) are asking for—focus, grounding, healing, or elevation.
- **Customize by Moon Phase:** Combine a calming strain like Northern Lights during a Pisces new moon, or energize a waxing Gemini moon with Sour Diesel.
- **Consider Your Natal Chart:** Your sun sign is key, but your moon and rising may guide your cannabis compatibility even more accurately.

Your strain is your *spiritual strain*. Choose it as you would choose your rituals: with sacred intention and cosmic curiosity.

Appendix B: Zodiac & Strain Compatibility Chart

Aligning your cannabis experience with your celestial blueprint

Your zodiac sign reveals more than personality—it uncovers how you best elevate, relax, reflect, and create. Cannabis, much like astrology, is a tool for tuning into different frequencies of self. This compatibility chart brings both worlds together, offering curated strain suggestions that enhance each sign's natural tendencies and support their highest version.

Each entry includes:

- **Zodiac Sign**
- **Recommended Strain**
- **Experience Focus** (what it amplifies or soothes)
- **Flavor Notes & Additional Ritual Use** (optional layer for holistic alignment)

⬦ **Aries – Jack Herer**

Experience Focus: Motivation, action, initiative

Why It Works: Aries is ruled by Mars—energetic, driven, sometimes impulsive. Jack Herer's sativa-forward buzz enhances ambition, courage, and quick-start enthusiasm.

Flavor Notes: Pine, citrus, spice

Suggested Ritual: Use for jumpstarting projects or morning movement meditations.

◈ Taurus – Granddaddy Purple

Experience Focus: Relaxation, luxury, indulgence

Why It Works: Taurus craves comfort and sensuality. GDP provides body-melting calm, enhancing everything from silk sheets to gourmet snacks.

Flavor Notes: Grape, berry, earthy musk

Suggested Ritual: Ideal for self-care nights, bath rituals, and sensory grounding.

◈ **Gemini – Sour Diesel**

Experience Focus: Conversation, curiosity, verbal agility

Why It Works: Ruled by Mercury, Gemini thrives on stimulation. Sour Diesel provides mental lift, talkativeness, and thought expansion.

Flavor Notes: Diesel, lemon, herbal

Suggested Ritual: Use for writing, podcasting, stoned debates, or socializing.

◈ Cancer – Blueberry

Experience Focus: Emotional balance, nostalgia, comfort

Why It Works: Cancers are deeply sensitive and sentimental. Blueberry soothes emotional tides while invoking a cozy, heart-opening calm.

Flavor Notes: Sweet berries, vanilla

Suggested Ritual: Blanket forts, memory journaling, or full moon reflections.

◈ **Leo – Super Lemon Haze**

Experience Focus: Spotlight energy, charisma, playfulness
Why It Works: Leo needs to shine. This strain boosts confidence and creativity, making Leo the life of any smoke circle.

Flavor Notes: Citrus, lemon zest, pepper

Suggested Ritual: Karaoke nights, art creation, or fire sign dance sessions.

⬖ Virgo – Harlequin

Experience Focus: Clarity, wellness, calm productivity

Why It Works: Virgo's analytical mind benefits from Harlequin's high-CBD balance—providing relaxation without disrupting focus or flow.

Flavor Notes: Earthy mango, pine

Suggested Ritual: Use during tidying rituals, skincare routines, or stress detox evenings.

◈ **Libra – Wedding Cake**

Experience Focus: Harmony, aesthetic pleasure, equilibrium

Why It Works: Venus-ruled Libra values beauty and balance. Wedding Cake's euphoric calm helps soften decision fatigue while enhancing ambiance.

Flavor Notes: Sweet vanilla, tangy earth

Suggested Ritual: Smoke before a romantic evening, music appreciation, or home decorating.

◈ **Scorpio – Purple Haze**

Experience Focus: Depth, transformation, mystery

Why It Works: Scorpio navigates shadows with passion. Purple Haze amplifies introspection, dream work, and emotional metamorphosis.

Flavor Notes: Grape candy, floral musk

Suggested Ritual: Tarot spreads, shadow journaling, or full sensory immersion experiences.

◈ **Sagittarius – Durban Poison**

Experience Focus: Exploration, open-mindedness, mental travel

Why It Works: Sag is the philosopher-adventurer. Durban Poison enhances mental clarity and expands boundaries, perfect for cosmic quests.

Flavor Notes: Sweet licorice, pine

Suggested Ritual: Use before traveling, hiking, or philosophical stargazing.

◈ Capricorn – Green Crack

Experience Focus: Ambition, productivity, vision

Why It Works: Capricorn's driven nature matches Green Crack's laser focus. It sharpens goals and supports tireless work without burnout.

Flavor Notes: Tropical fruit, citrus

Suggested Ritual: Planning sessions, business idea sketching, or grounded manifestation.

◈ Aquarius – Chocolope

Experience Focus: Innovation, futurism, social thinking

Why It Works: Aquarius is forward-thinking and unconventional. Chocolope ignites visionary thoughts and radical creativity.

Flavor Notes: Chocolate, earthy coffee, sweet spice

Suggested Ritual: Brainstorming for change, social cause planning, or solo invention sessions.

◈ **Pisces – Northern Lights**

Experience Focus: Dreamscape, imagination, emotional release

Why It Works: Pisces lives between dimensions. Northern Lights slows the body and opens portals to fantasy, creativity, and inner peace.

Flavor Notes: Pine, mint, honey musk

Suggested Ritual: Bedtime rituals, lucid dreaming prep, or sacred playlist creation.

◈ **Final Notes on Compatibility**

- **Layer with Moon & Rising Signs:** Your full astrological chart may refine your perfect strain even further.
- **Adapt for Seasons:** Earth signs may enjoy sativas in summer; air signs may seek hybrids during grounding fall months.
- **Honor the Intention:** These pairings are invitations—not pre-scriptions. Listen to your body, your mood, and your stars.

Your cannabis ritual is your celestial ritual. The stars have spoken—now let them *spark*.

<u>Message from the Author:</u>

I hope you enjoyed this book, I love astrology and knew there was not a book such as this out on the shelf. I love metaphysical items as well. Please check out my other books:

-Life of Government Benefits

-My life of Hell

-My life with Hydrocephalus

-Red Sky

-World Domination:Woman's rule

-World Domination:Woman's Rule 2: The War

-Life and Banishment of Apophis: book 1

-The Kidney Friendly Diet

-The Ultimate Hemp Cookbook

-Creating a Dispensary(legally)

-Cleanliness throughout life: the importance of showering from childhood to adulthood.

-Strong Roots: The Risks of Overcoddling children

-Hemp Horoscopes: Cosmic Insights and Earthly Healing

- Celestial Hemp Navigating the Zodiac: Through the Green Cosmos

-Astrological Hemp: Aligning The Stars with Earth's Ancient Herb

-The Astrological Guide to Hemp: Stars, Signs, and Sacred Leaves

-Green Growth: Innovative Marketing Strategies for your Hemp Products and Dispensary

-Cosmic Cannabis

-Astrological Munchies

-Henry The Hemp

-Zodiacal Roots: The Astrological Soul Of Hemp

- **Green Constellations: Intersection of Hemp and Zodiac**

-Hemp in The Houses: An astrological Adventure Through The Cannabis Galaxy

-Galactic Ganja Guide

Heavenly Hemp
Zodiac Leaves
Doctor Who Astrology
Cannastrology
Stellar Satvias and Cosmic Indicas
Celestial Cannabis: A Zodiac Journey
AstroHerbology: The Sky and The Soil: Volume 1
AstroHerbology:Celestial Cannabis:Volume 2
Cosmic Cannabis Cultivation
The Starry Guide to Herbal Harmony: Volume 1
The Starry Guide to Herbal Harmony: Cannabis Universe: Volume 2

Yugioh Astrology: Astrological Guide to Deck, Duels and more
Nightmare Mansion: Echoes of The Abyss
Nightmare Mansion 2: Legacy of Shadows
Nightmare Mansion 3: Shadows of the Forgotten
Nightmare Mansion 4: Echoes of the Damned
The Life and Banishment of Apophis: Book 2
Nightmare Mansion: Halls of Despair
Healing with Herb: Cannabis and Hydrocephalus
Planetary Pot: Aligning with Astrological Herbs: Volume 1
Fast Track to Freedom: 30 Days to Financial Independence Using AI, Assets, and Agile Hustles
Cosmic Hemp Pathways
How to Become Financially Free in 30 Days: 10,000 Paths to Prosperity
Zodiacal Herbage: Astrological Insights: Volume 1
Nightmare Mansion: Whispers in the Walls
The Daleks Invade Atlantis
Henry the hemp and Hydrocephalus

10X The Kidney Friendly Diet
Cannabis Universe: Adult coloring book

Hemp Astrology: The Healing Power of the Stars

Zodiacal Herbage: Astrological Insights: Cannabis Universe: Volume 2

Planetary Pot: Aligning with Astrological Herbs: Cannabis Universes: Volume 2

Doctor Who: Convergence Protocol – The Replicator War

Nightmare Mansion: Curse of the Blood Moon

The Celestial Stoner: A Guide to the Zodiac

Cosmic Pleasures: Sex Toy Astrology for Every Sign

Hydrocephalus Astrology: Navigating the Stars and Healing Waters

Lapis and the Mischievous Chocolate Bar

Celestial Positions: Sexual Astrology for Every Sign

Apophis's Shadow Work Journal: : A Journey of Self-Discovery and Healing

Kinky Cosmos: Sexual Kink Astrology for Every Sign

Digital Cosmos: The Astrological Digimon Compendium

Stellar Seeds: The Cosmic Guide to Growing with Astrology

Apophis's Daily Gratitude Journal

Cat Astrology: Feline Mysteries of the Cosmos

The Cosmic Kama Sutra: An Astrological Guide to Sexual Positions

Unleash Your Potential: A Guided Journal Powered by AI Insights

Whispers of the Enchanted Grove

Cosmic Pleasures: An Astrological Guide to Sexual Kinks

369, 12 Manifestation Journal

Whisper of the nocturne journal(blank journal for writing or drawing)

The Boogey Book

Locked In Reflection: A Chastity Journey Through Locktober

Generating Wealth Quickly:How to Generate $100,000 in 24 Hours

Star Magic: Harness the Power of the Universe

The Flatulence Chronicles: A Fart Journal for Self-Discovery

The Doctor and The Death Moth

Seize the Day: A Personal Seizure Tracking Journal

The Ultimate Boogeyman Safari: A Journey into the Boogie World and Beyond

Whispers of Samhain: 1,000 Spells of Love, Luck, and Lunar Magic: Samhain Spell Book

Apophis's guides:Witch's Spellbook Crafting Guide for Halloween

<u>Frost & Flame: The Enchanted Yule Grimoire of 1000 Winter Spells</u>

<u>The Ultimate Boogey Goo Guide & Spooky Activities for Halloween Fun</u>

Harmony of the Scales: A Libra's Spellcraft for Balance and Beauty

The Enchanted Advent: 36 Days of Christmas Wonders

Nightmare Mansion: The Labyrinth of Screams

Harvest of Enchantment: 1,000 Spells of Gratitude, Love, and Fortune for Thanksgiving

The Boogey Chronicles: A Journal of Nightly Encounters and Shadowy Secrets

The 12 Days of Financial Freedom: A Step-by-Step Christmas Countdown to Transform Your Finances

Sigil of the Eternal Spiral Blank Journal

A Christmas Feast: Timeless Recipes for Every Meal

Holiday Stress-Free Solutions: A Survival Guide to Thriving During the Festive Season

Yu-Gi-Oh! Holiday Gifting Mastery: The Ultimate Guide for Fans and Newcomers Alike

Holiday Harmony: A Hydrocephalus Survival Guide for the Festive Season

Celestial Craft: The Witch's Almanac for 2025 – A Cosmic Guide to Manifestations, Moons, and Mystical Events

Doctor Who: The Toymaker's Winter Wonderland

Tulsa King Unveiled: A Thrilling Guide to Stallone's Mafia Masterpiece

Pendulum Craft: A Complete Guide to Crafting and Using Personalized Divination Tools

Nightmare Mansion: Santa's Eternal Eve

Starlight Noel: A Cosmic Journey through Christmas Mysteries

The Dark Architect: Unlocking the Blueprint of Existence

Surviving the Embrace: The Ultimate Guide to Encounters with The Hugging Molly

The Enchanted Codex: Secrets of the Craft for Witches, Wiccans, and Pagans

Harvest of Gratitude: A Complete Thanksgiving Guide

Yuletide Essentials: A Complete Guide to an Authentic and Magical Christmas

Celestial Smokes: A Cosmic Guide to Cigars and Astrology

Living in Balance: A Comprehensive Survival Guide to Thriving with Diabetes Insipidus

Cosmic Symbiosis: The Venom Zodiac Chronicles

The Cursed Paw of Ambition

Cosmic Symbiosis: The Astrological Venom Journal

Celestial Wonders Unfold: A Stargazer's Guide to the Cosmos (2024-2029)

The Ultimate Black Friday Prepper's Guide: Mastering Shopping Strategies and Savings

Cosmic Sales: The Astrological Guide to Black Friday Shopping

Legends of the Corn Mother and Other Harvest Myths

Whispers of the Harvest: The Corn Mother's Journal

The Evergreen Spellbook

The Doctor Meets the Boogeyman

The White Witch of Rose Hall's SpellBook

The Gingerbread Golem's Shadow: A Study in Sweet Darkness

The Gingerbread Golem Codex: An Academic Exploration of Sweet Myths

The Gingerbread Golem Grimoire: Sweet Magicks and Spells for the Festive Witch

The Curse of the Gingerbread Golem

10-minute Christmas Crafts for kids

<u>Christmas Crisis Solutions: The Ultimate Last-Minute Survival Guide</u>

Gingerbread Golem Recipes: Holiday Treats with a Magical Twist

The Infinite Key: Unlocking Mystical Secrets of the Ages

Enchanted Yule: A Wiccan and Pagan Guide to a Magical and Memorable Season

Dinosaurs of Power: Unlocking Ancient Magick

Astro-Dinos: The Cosmic Guide to Prehistoric Wisdom

Gallifrey's Yule Logs: A Festive Doctor Who Cookbook

The Dino Grimoire: Secrets of Prehistoric Magick

The Gift They Never Knew They Needed

The Gingerbread Golem's Culinary Alchemy: Enchanting Recipes for a Sweetly Dark Feast

A Time Lord Christmas: Holiday Adventures with the Doctor

Krampusproofing Your Home: Defensive Strategies for Yule

Silent Frights: A Collection of Christmas Creepypastas to Chill Your Bones

Santa Raptor's Jolly Carnage: A Dino-Claus Christmas Tale

Prehistoric Palettes: A Dino Wicca Coloring Journey

The Christmas Wishkeeper Chronicles

The Starlight Sleigh: A Holiday Journey

Elf Secrets: The True Magic of the North Pole

Candy Cane Conjurations

Cooking with Kids: Recipes Under 20 Minutes

Doctor Who: The TARDIS Confiscation

The Anxiety First Aid Kit: Quick Tools to Calm Your Mind

Frosty Whispers: A Winter's Tale

The Infinite Key: Unlocking the Secrets to Prosperity, Resilience, and Purpose

The Grasping Void: Why You'll Regret This Purchase

Astrology for Busy Bees: Star Signs Simplified

The Instant Focus Formula: Cut Through the Noise

The Secret Language of Colors: Unlocking the Emotional Codes

Sacred Fossil Chronicles: Blank Journal

The Christmas Cottage Miracle

Feeding Frenzy: Graboid-Inspired Recipes

Manifest in Minutes: The Quick Law of Attraction Guide

The Symbiote Chronicles: Doctor Who's Venomous Journey

Think Tiny, Grow Big: The Minimalist Mindset

The Energy Key: Unlocking Limitless Motivation

New Year, New Magic: Manifesting Your Best Year Yet

Unstoppable You: Mastering Confidence in Minutes

Infinite Energy: The Secret to Never Feeling Drained

Lightning Focus: Mastering the Art of Productivity in a Distracted World

Saturnalia Manifestation Magick: A Guide to Unlocking Abundance During the Solstice

Graboids and Garland: The Ultimate Tremors-Themed Christmas Guide

12 Nights of Holiday Magic

The Power of Pause: 60-Second Mindfulness Practices

The Quick Reset: How to Reclaim Your Life After Burnout

The Shadow Eater: A Tale of Despair and Survival

The Micro-Mastery Method: Transform Your Skills in Just Minutes a Day

Reclaiming Time: How to Live More by Doing Less

Chronovore: The Eternal Nexus

The Mind Reset: Unlocking Your Inner Peace in a Chaotic World

Confidence Code: Building Unshakable Self-Belief

Baby the Vampire Terrier

Baby the Vampire Terrier's Christmas Adventure

Celestial Streams: The Content Creator's Astrology Manual

The Wealth Whisperer: Unlocking Abundance with Everyday Actions

The Energy Equation: Maximize Your Output Without Burning Out

The Happiness Algorithm: Science-Backed Steps to Joyful Living

Stress-Free Success: Achieving Goals Without Anxiety

Mindful Wealth: The New Blueprint for Financial Freedom

The Festive Flavors of New Year: A Culinary Celebration

The Master's Gambit: Keys of Eternal Power

Shadowed Secrets: Groundhog Day Mysteries

Beneath the Burrow: Lessons from the Groundhog

Spring's Whispers: The Groundhog's Prediction

The Limitless Mindset: Unlock Your Untapped Potential

The Focus Funnel: How to Cut Through Chaos and Get Results

Bold Moves: Building Courage to Live on Your Terms

The Daily Shift: Simple Practices for Lasting Transformation

The Quarter-Life Reset: Thriving in Your 20s and 30s

The Art of Shadowplay: Building Your Own Personal Myth

The Eternal Loop: Finding Purpose in Repetition

Burrowing Wisdom: Life Lessons from the Groundhog

Shadow Work: A Groundhog Day Perspective

Love in Bloom: 5-Minute Romantic Gestures

The Shadowspell Codex: Secrets of Forbidden Magick

The Burnout Cure: Finding Balance in a Busy World

The Groundhog Prophecy: Unlocking Seasonal Secrets

Nog Tales: The Spirited History of Eggnog

Six More Weeks: Embracing Seasonal Transitions

The Lumivian Chronicles: Fragments of the Fifth Dimension

Money on Your Mind: A Beginner's Guide to Wealth
The Focus Fix: Breaking Through Distraction
January's Spirit Keepers: Mystical Protectors of the Cold
Creativity Unchained: Unlocking Your Wildest Ideas in 2025
Manifestation Mastery: 365 Days to Rewrite Your Reality
The Groundhog's Mirror: Reflecting on Change
The Weeping Angels' Christmas Curse
Burrowed in Time: A Groundhog Day Journey
Heartbeats: Poems to Share with Your Valentine
Dino Wicca: The Sacred Grimoire of Prehistoric Magick
Courage of the Pride: Finding Your Inner Roar
The Lion's Leap: Bold Moves for Big Results
Healthy Hustle: Achieving Without Overworking
Practical Manifesting: Turning Dreams into Reality in 2025
Jurassic Pharaohs: Unlocking the Magick of Ancient Egypt and Dino Wicca
The Happiness Equation: Small Changes for Big Joy
The Confidence Compass: Finding Your Inner Strength
Whispers in the Hollow: Tales of the Forgotten Beasts
Echoes from the Hollow: The Return of Forgotten Beasts
The Hollow Ascendant: The Rise of the Forgotten Beasts
The Relationship Reset: Building Better Connections
Mastering the Morning: How to Win the Day Before 8 AM
The Shadow's Dance: Groundhog Day Symbolism
Cupid's Kitchen: Quick Valentine's Day Recipes
Valentine's Day on a Budget: Love Without Breaking the Bank
Astrocraft: Aligning the Stars in the World of Minecraft
Forecasting Life: Groundhog Day Reflections
Bleeding Hearts: Twisted Tales of Valentine's Terror
Herbal Smoke Revolution: The Ultimate Guide to Nature's Cigarette Alternative
Winter's Wrath: The Complete Survival Blueprint for Extreme Freezes.

The Leprechaun's Guide to Wealth and Wisdom

Dancing with the Sidhe: Celebrating the Otherworld

Shamrocks and Shadows: Mysteries of the Green Isle

Emerald Energy: Harnessing Luck and Growth

The Gingerbread Golem's Valentine: A Sweetheart's Guide to Love and Enchantment

The Celtic Knot: Weaving Life and Destiny

Green Fire: Elemental Magic for St. Patrick's Day

Clover Chronicles: Finding Your Inner Luck

Ireland's Mystical Creatures: A Field Guide

Gingerbread Golem's Love Almanac

Prowl and Thrive: The Lion's Guide to Success

Love Alchemy: Transforming Your Life Through Heart Energy

WORLD DOMINATION: Woman's Rule 3:The New Life

The Midnight Rose: A Guide to Lunar Love Spells

The Forbidden Letters: Writing Your Own Love Prophecy

Luck and Lore: St. Patrick's Day for Modern Mystics

The Green Path: A Pagan Celebration of Renewal

The Dark Architect's Guide to Reprogramming Reality

Prankster's Paradise: A Guide to Harmless Hijinks

Manifest Your Reality: The Law of Attraction Simplified

The TARDIS Owner's Manual: Understanding the Doctor's Ship: *A complete guide to the TARDIS, its technology, secrets, and mysteries*

Starlit Romance: Astrology Secrets for Finding True Love

The Time Lord's Atlas: A Complete Guide to the Whoniverse: *A breakdown of the locations, planets, and dimensions explored in Doctor Who*

Sweetheart Shadows: The Dark Side of Love and Attraction

February Fire: Reigniting Passion in Every Area of Life

The Self-Love Toolkit: 5 Ways to Embrace Who You Are

February Sparks: Ignite Your Dreams in 28 Days

March to Success: A 31-Day Action Blueprint
Ancient Paths: The 13 Sacred Principles of Dino Wicca
Echoes of Tomorrow: Navigating the AI Revolution
The Wellness Blueprint: Balancing Mind, Body, and Soul
Green Horizons: Sustainable Living for a Better Tomorrow
The AI Wealth Code: How to Make Millions with Automation
AI-Powered Creativity: Writing, Art, and Music for Profit
Extinction Rites: Rebirthing Your Soul Through Prehistoric Magick
Sacred Serpents tarot
Celestial Enchantment blank journal
Star Strains
Culinary Journeys: Exploring Global Flavors at Home
The Hollowvale Curse
The Hollowvale Harvest
The Egg of Transformation: Awakening Your Inner Power
Blooming Into Power: A Wiccan Guide to Spring Awakening
The Nightmare Nexus: The Third Doctor's Perilous Haunting
Digital Detox: Reclaiming Your Life in a Connected World
Ostara's Path: Walking the Spiral of Renewal
The Sacred Hare
Financial Freedom: Building Wealth in the Modern Age
Spring's Cauldron: Stirring the Waters of Change
The Hollowvale Pact
Quantum Consciousness: The Science of Reality Shifting
The Hollowvale Hunger
The Sacred Waters Within: A Witch's Guide to Hydrocephalus Magick
The Raven's Nest: Building a Life of Unshakable Stability
AI and the Human Mind: The Future of Intelligence
The Hollowvale Reckoning
Timeless Love: Building and Maintaining Lasting Relationships

The Magick of Motherhood: Reclaiming Your Power Through Rituals

The Pagan Path to Self-Love: A Goddess's Guide to Worth and Confidence

Wild Woman Magick: Unleashing Your Primal Power

The Money Magnet Blueprint: Unlocking Unlimited Wealth

Biohacking 101: Unlock Your Body's Full Potential

The Wild Father: A Pagan Guide to Strength and Wisdom

The Sacred Masculine: Unlocking Your Inner Power

The Druid's Compass

The Warrior's Mindset

The Father's Fire

Odin's Path

Ancestral Bonds

The House That Whispers

The Magician's Code

The Wild Hunt

The Green Man's Path

The Altar of Success

The Shadow and the Sword

The High Priestess's Guide to Energy Healing

The Lunar Mother

The Sacred Self-Care Grimoire

The Womb Wisdom Codex

The Wheel of the Mother

The Witch's Guide to Manifestation

The Q2 Reset

The Ultimate Guide to AI-Powered Passive Income

Escape the 9-5

AI Feline Fortunes

The Tear-Stained Grimoire

Razorblade Runes

Cemetery Sirens

The Midnight Wristwatch
The Town That Forgets
AI Horror & Creepypasta
The Hollow Frequency
The Breach Echo
The Quiet Between Worlds
The Sigil of Tharan-Khul
Summon the Vault of Y'ha'ten
The Becoming Codex
The Profit of Az'ra-nar
The Drowned Logos
Echoes of the Eldritch Will
The Deep Ledger
Necronomicon of Networth
Covenant of the Wealthwyrm
The Whisperer's Manifesto
The Rites of Azh-K'luth
The Ark of the Crawling Coin
The Tithe of Shadows
Inkheart Abyss
The Timewinds of Y'ha-nthlei
The Spiral Labyrinth of Azag-Nirrh
The Gallifreyan Heresy of the Black Pharaoh
The Psalms of Nyog-Sotha
Black Rain Alchemy
The Infinite Maw
The Entropic Blueprint
The Oracle of Sh'guul
The Book of Breach
The Drowned Saint's Testament
Dreamcraft of the Sleeper God
The Silence Market
Cthonomics: The Dark Wealth Algorithm

Invocation of the Ten-Eyed King
Wealthbound to the Wyrm Below
Become the Unnameable
Codex of the Sovereign Flame
Rituals of Relentless Becoming
The Shadow Ascends
The Eyes Beneath You
The Will That Wakes Worlds
Silence Is a Weapon
The Mirror That Screams
The Whisper Between Moments
The Mind That Devours Fear
The Myth of the Finished Self
The Architect of Your Madness
The Voice You've Buried
The Discipline of Madness
Stormborn: Awakening Your Inner Tempest
The Mind That Ate Time
Unbind Your Becoming
The Pact You Owe Yourself
The Devourer's Diet
The Acid That Carves the Path
The Tower You Must Burn
The Breath Between Worlds
Speak Like the Deep
The Labyrinth Within
The Spine of the Sea God
Rejection Is a Portal
The Crown You Refused
The Scar Is the Spell
The Lightless Flame
The Habit of Becoming Horrific
ChickenJockey Chaos

The Gatekeeper Within

You Are Not Your Name

The Compass of the Mad

The Archive of Unsent Letters

What the Mirror Can't Show You

The Knife You Needed

Worship Nothing, Become Everything

The Other Voice

The Body the World Forgot

The Vein of the Void

The Black Bone Codex

The Puzzle of the Hidden Self (Millennium Puzzle)

The Eye That Sees the Lie *(Millennium Eye)*

The Ring of Return (Millennium Ring)

The Rod of Relentless Will *(Millennium Rod)*

The Tally of the Soul (Millennium Tauk/Necklace)

The Key to the Locked Timeline (Millennium Key)

The Scale of Sacred Decisions (Millennium Scales)

Inferno Bites: The UnOfficial Minecraft Lava Cookbook

Rot in the Attic

Prana: The Hidden Force of Your Infinite Self

The Shadow Realm Within: Transforming Darkness Into Destiny

The Borderland Collapse

Claws of Protection: Bastet's Defensive Magick

Mr. Ring-a-Ding's Madness

Yugioh Astrology: Celestial Deckcraft and Duel Destiny (2026–2027 Edition)

The Seal You Signed: Unlocking the Power You Once Feared

The Puzzle of Infinite Minds: Unlocking the Mentalism Hidden Within

The Eye That Mirrors the All: Secrets of Inner Reflection

Doctor Who: The Toymaker's Broadcast

Rootwake: The Carbon Covenant

Skitter Logic: Unlearning the Fear That Built You

Doctor Who: The World That Froths

Rootwake: The Fizz That Rewrites Flesh

Rootwake: Frothfather of the World

The Holly Pact: Blood Beneath the Mistletoe

The 2nd Mass Principle: Building Unbreakable Tribes

Web of Wits: A Survival Guide to Encounters with Anasi the Spider (Aunt Nancy)

The Hexbreaking Handbook: Effective Spells to Remove Curses

Pop Alchemy: Transform Your Life One Sip at a Time

The Mason Code: Leading in Unleadable Times

Petosiris and the Fifth Chamber of Thoth

The Ether Seed Within

The Parent of Tomorrow

Petosiris's Pyramid of Perpetual Wealth

Unlearn the World

Grimoire of the Hollow Tongue

Zodiac Weeds: Finding Your Strain Through the Stars

Aquarius Rises in the Bank

The Sugar God's Smile

The Skinclock Reversal: Biohacking the Face of Time

Debtburn: How to Obliterate What You Owe Forever

The Ice Cream Oracle: What Your Cone Says About Your Future

Silence Is Sovereignty: The Power of Being Unreadable

The Wind That Whispers Through Stone

Path of the Four Directions

Doctor Who: The Maestro's Symphony of Endings

Oxygen Grail: Breathing to Undo the Clock

Zodiacal Collapse: When Stars Devour Time

Teachings from the Red Sand Silence

Doctor Who: Omega – The Broken Equation
Memory Wipe Your Past: Start Over Like a MiB
Mitochondria Prime: Ignite the Core of Youth
A Nest of Roaches
Grub from the Galaxy: MiB Recipes You'll Never Forget
Whiskers of Power: Bastet's Guide to Inner Sovereignty
The Gift Must Cost Them: Negotiation Through Unequal Exchange
The Worm Guys' Wealth Code: Hustle Like an Alien
Bug Out: The Edgar Method for Ruthless Goal Setting
Weaving Life with Spiderwoman's Pattern
Doctor Who: The Rani's Renaissance
How to Get a Job (If You're a Puppygirl)

Get Some Tarot cards: https://www.makeplayingcards.com/sell/ apophis-occult-shop

Get   some   shirts: https://www.bonfire.com/store/apophis-shirt-emporium/

<u>**Instagrams:**</u>
@apophis_enterprises,
@apophisbookemporium,
@apophisscardshop
Twitter: @apophisenterpr1
Tiktok:@apophisenterprise
Youtube: @sg1fan23477
Hive: @sg1fan23477
CheeLee: @SG1fan23477

Podcast: Apophis Chat Zone: https://open.spotify.com/show/5zXbrCLEV2xzCp8ybrfHsk?si=fb4d4fdbdce44dec

Newsletter: https://apophiss-newsletter-27c897.beehiiv.com/

If you want to support me or see posts of other projects that I have come over to: **buymeacoffee.com/mpetchinskg**
I post there daily several times a day

Get your Dinowicca or Christmas themed digital products, especially Santa Raptor songs and other musics. Here: **https://sg1fan23477.gumroad.com**

Apophis Yuletide Digital has not only digital Christmas items, but it will have all things with Dinowicca as well as other Digital products.